UKULELE
SHEET MUSIC 2010–2019

ISBN 978-1-5400-9173-4

Visit Hal Leonard Online at
www.halleonard.com

Contact us:
Hal Leonard
7777 West Bluemound Road
Milwaukee, WI 53213
Email: info@halleonard.com

In Europe, contact:
Hal Leonard Europe Limited
42 Wigmore Street
Marylebone, London, W1U 2RN
Email: info@halleonardeurope.com

In Australia, contact:
Hal Leonard Australia Pty. Ltd.
4 Lentara Court
Cheltenham, Victoria, 3192 Australia
Email: info@halleonard.com.au

CONTENTS

All About That Bass

Words and Music by Kevin Kadish and Meghan Trainor

First note

Chorus
Moderately fast

C

Be - cause you know I'm all a - bout that bass, 'bout that

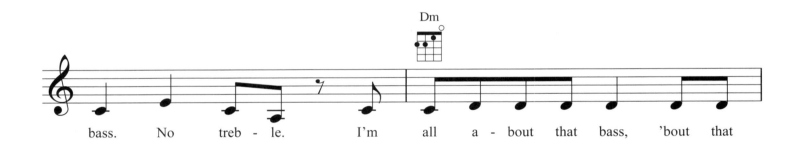

Dm

bass. No treb - le. I'm all a - bout that bass, 'bout that

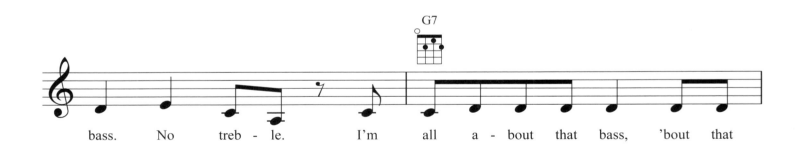

G7

bass. No treb - le. I'm all a - bout that bass, 'bout that

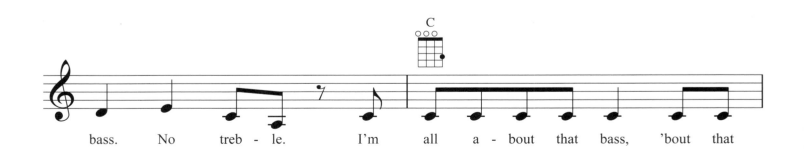

C

bass. No treb - le. I'm all a - bout that bass, 'bout that

Verse

N.C.

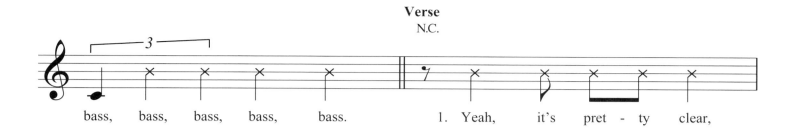

bass, bass, bass, bass, bass. 1. Yeah, it's pret - ty clear,

I ain't no size two. But I can shake it, shake it

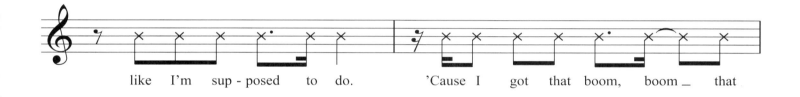

like I'm sup - posed to do. 'Cause I got that boom, boom __ that

all the boys chase and all _____ the right junk in all ___

C

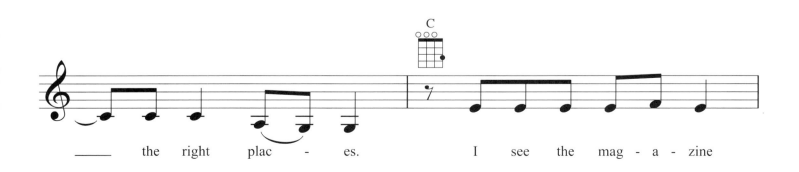

___ the right plac - es. I see the mag - a - zine

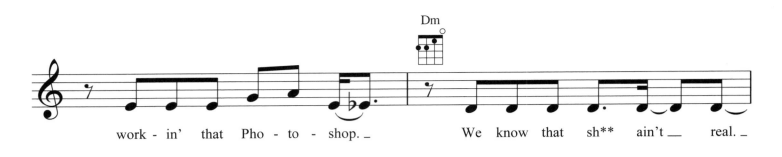

work - in' that Pho - to - shop. _ We know that sh** ain't _ real. _

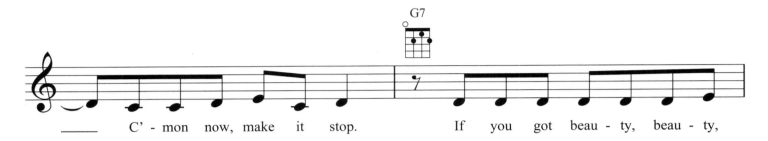

_ C' - mon now, make it stop. If you got beau - ty, beau - ty,

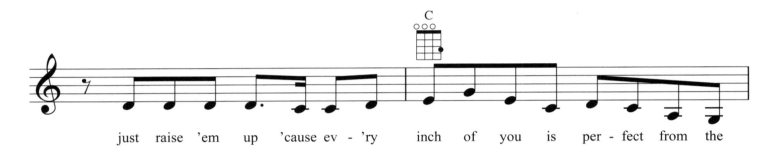

just raise 'em up 'cause ev - 'ry inch of you is per - fect from the

𝄋 Pre-Chorus

bot - tom to the top. Yeah, my ma - ma, _ she told me, _ "Don't

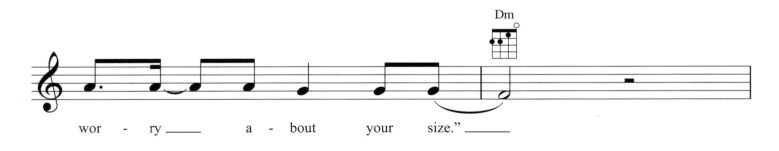

wor - ry _ a - bout your size." _

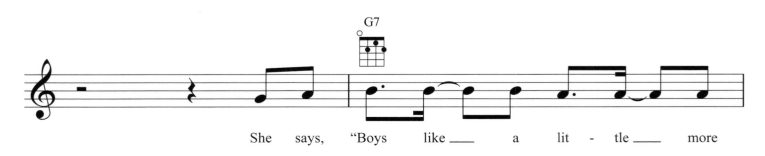

She says, "Boys like _ a lit - tle _ more

6

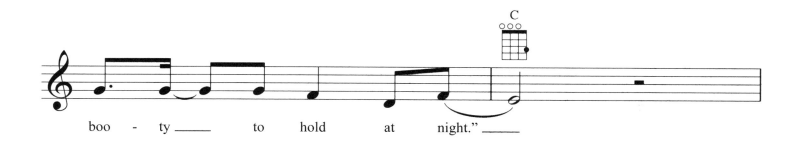

boo - ty _____ to hold at night." _____

You know I won't be _____ no stick fig - ure,

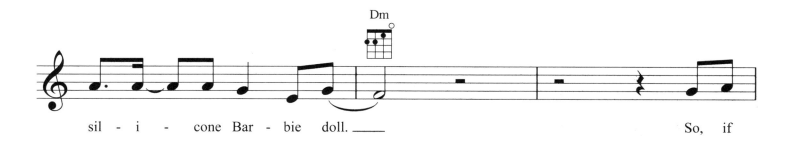

sil - i - cone Bar - bie doll. _____ So, if

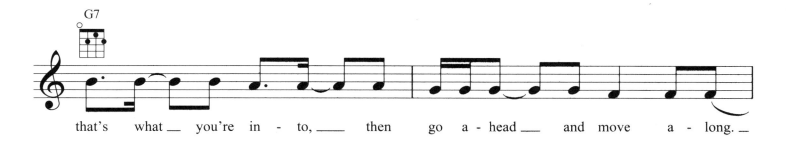

that's what _____ you're in - to, _____ then go a - head _____ and move a - long. _____

_____ Be - cause you know I'm

Chorus

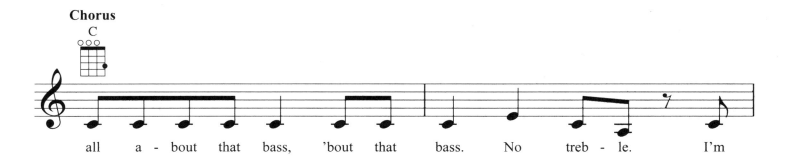

all a - bout that bass, 'bout that bass. No treb - le. I'm

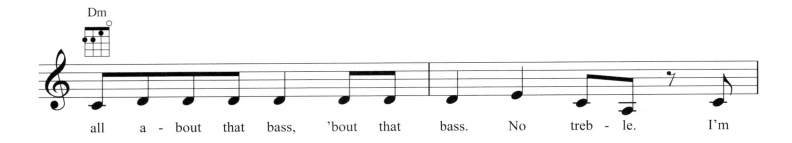

all a - bout that bass, 'bout that bass. No treb - le. I'm

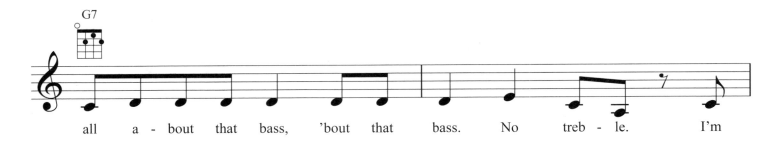

all a - bout that bass, 'bout that bass. No treb - le. I'm

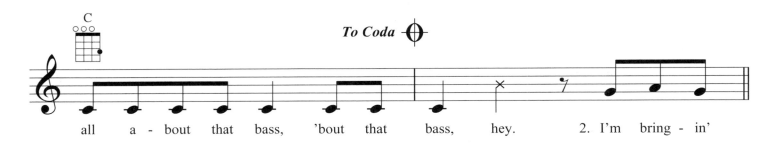

To Coda

all a - bout that bass, 'bout that bass, hey. 2. I'm bring - in'

Verse

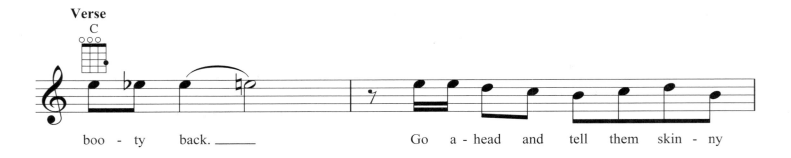

boo - ty back. _____ Go a - head and tell them skin - ny

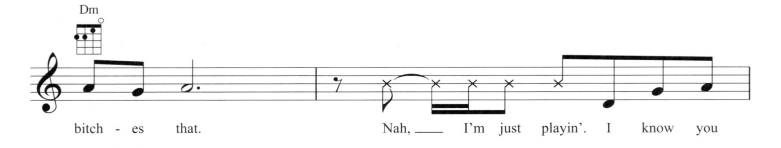

bitch - es that. Nah, _____ I'm just playin'. I know you

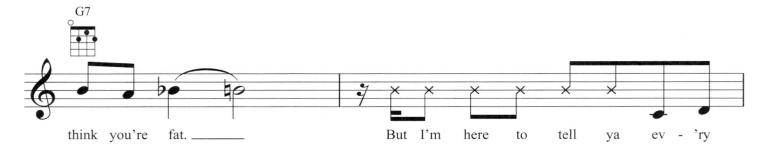

think you're fat. _____ But I'm here to tell ya ev - 'ry

8

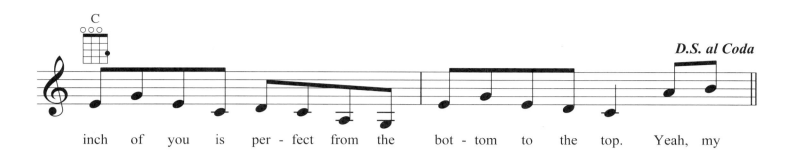

inch of you is per - fect from the bot - tom to the top. Yeah, my

Outro-Chorus

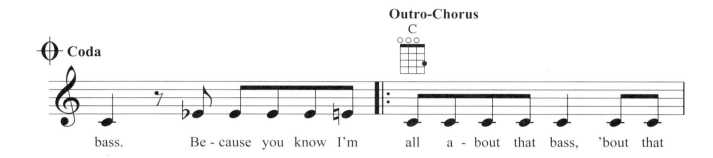

bass. Be - cause you know I'm all a - bout that bass, 'bout that

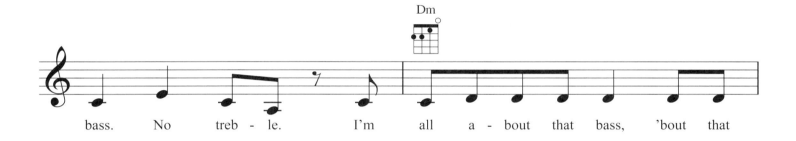

bass. No treb - le. I'm all a - bout that bass, 'bout that

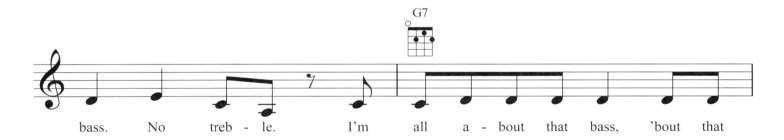

bass. No treb - le. I'm all a - bout that bass, 'bout that

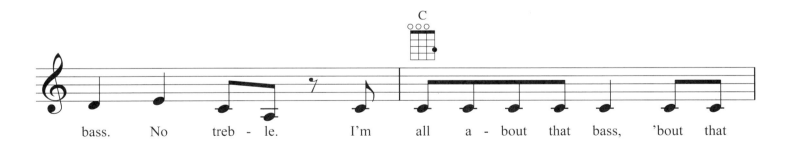

bass. No treb - le. I'm all a - bout that bass, 'bout that

bass. Be - cause you know I'm bass.

All of Me

Words and Music by John Stephens and Toby Gad

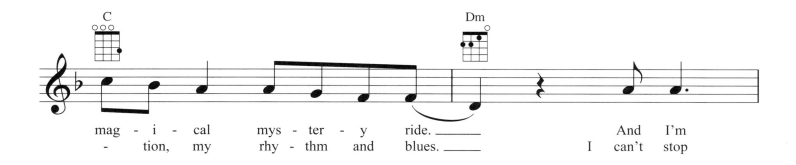

mag - i - cal   mys - ter - y   ride. _____   And   I'm
- tion,   my   rhy - thm   and   blues. _____   I   can't   stop

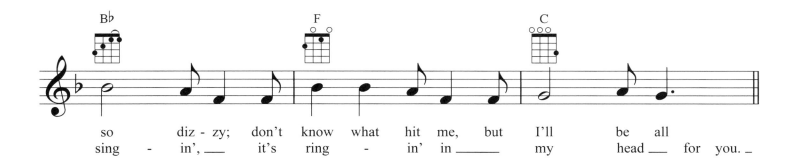

so   diz - zy;   don't   know   what   hit   me,   but   I'll   be   all
sing - in', ___   it's   ring - in'   in _____   my   head ___   for   you. _

Pre-Chorus

_____   right.}   My   head's   un - der   wa - ter, _____   but   I'm _

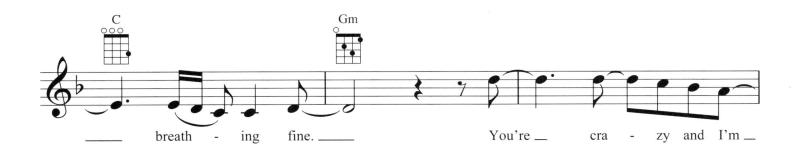

_____   breath - ing   fine. _____   You're ___   cra - zy   and   I'm _

_____   out ___   of   my   mind. _____   'Cause

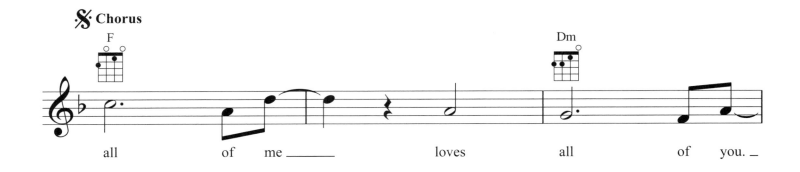

all   of me _____   loves   all   of   you. _

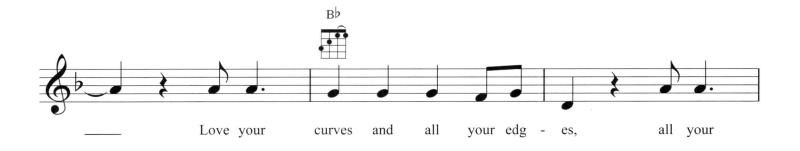

_____   Love your   curves   and   all   your   edg - es,   all   your

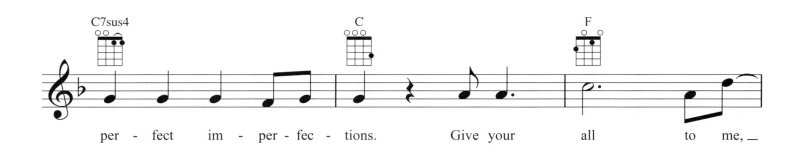

per - fect   im - per - fec - tions.   Give   your   all   to   me, _

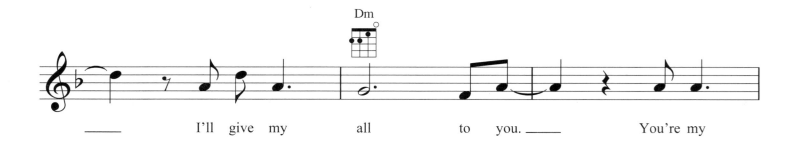

_____   I'll   give   my   all   to   you. _____   You're   my

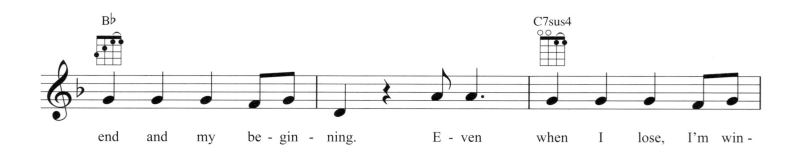

end   and   my   be - gin - ning.   E - ven   when   I   lose,   I'm   win-

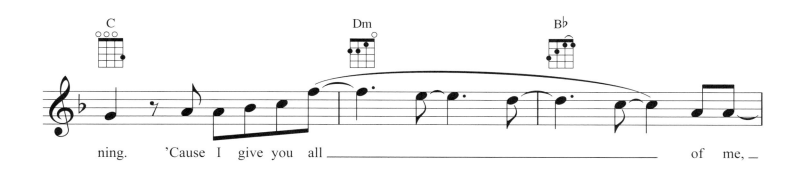

ning. 'Cause I give you all _____ of me, _

_____ and you give me all _____

_____ of you, _____ oh. _____

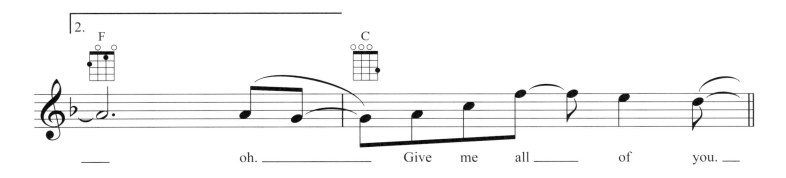

____ oh. _____ Give me all _____ of you. ____

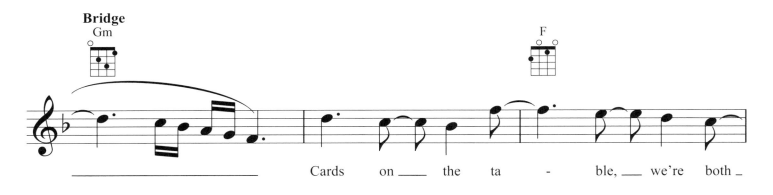

_____ Cards on ____ the ta - ble, ____ we're both _

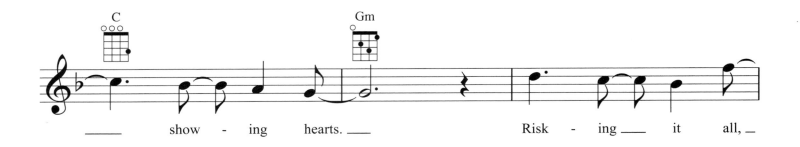

show - ing hearts. ____ Risk - ing ____ it all, ____

D.S. al Coda   Coda

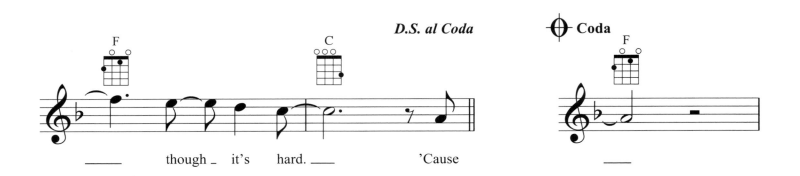

____ though _ it's hard. ____ 'Cause   ____

Outro

I give you all _____ of me, _

____   and you give me all _____

_____ of you, ____   oh. _____

Be Alright

Words and Music by Dean Lewis and Jon Cobbe Hume

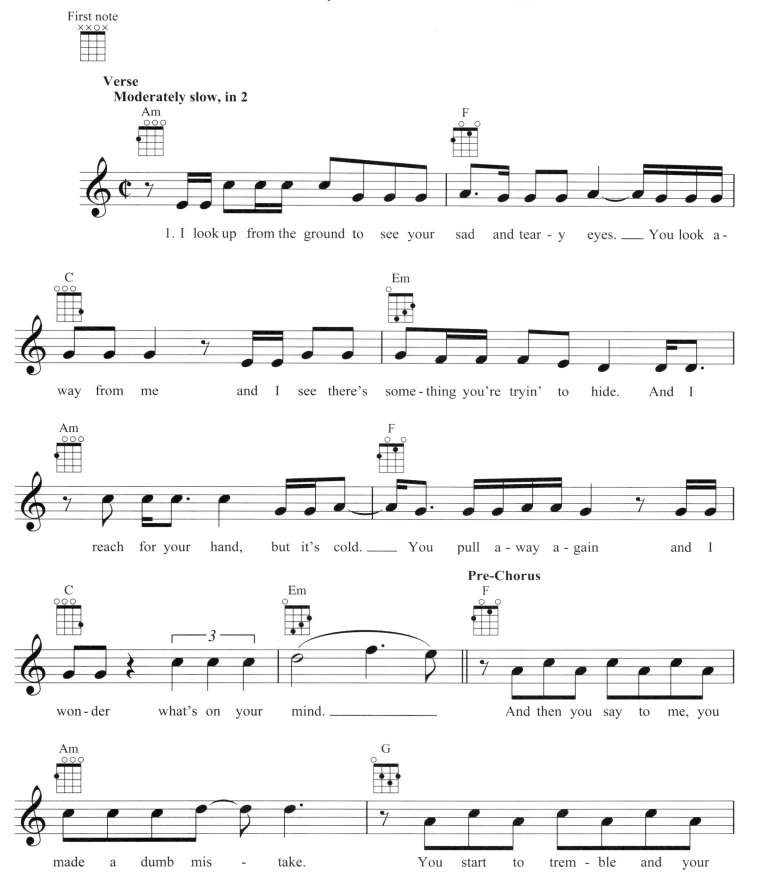

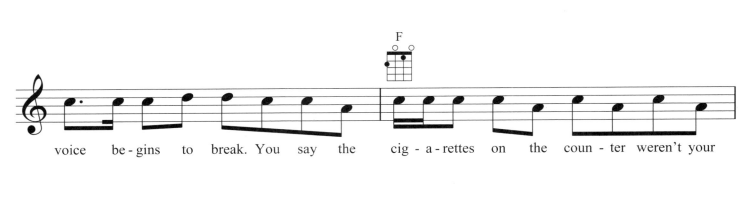

voice be - gins to break. You say the cig - a - rettes on the coun - ter weren't your

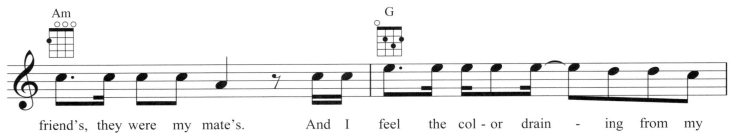

friend's, they were my mate's. And I feel the col - or drain - ing from my

Chorus

face. And my friends say: __ I know you love her, but it's

o - ver, mate. It does - n't mat - ter; put the phone a - way. _____

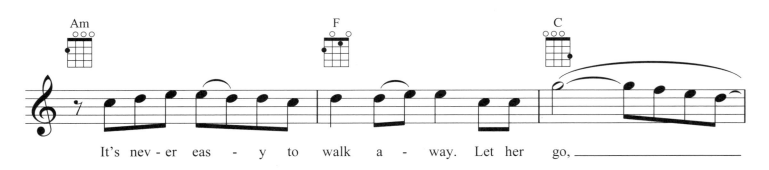

It's nev - er eas - y to walk a - way. Let her go, _____

Verse

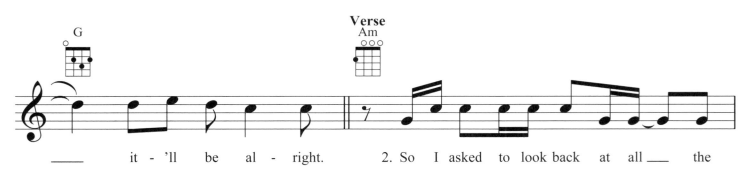

_____ it - 'll be al - right. 2. So I asked to look back at all __ the

mes-sag - es ____ you'd sent, and I know it was-n't right, __ but it was

fuck-ing with my _____ head. And ev -'ry-thing de - let - ed like the

past, yeah, it was gone. And when I touched _ your face, I ____ could

Pre-Chorus

tell you're mov - ing on. But it's not the fact that __ you

kissed him yes - ter - day, it's the feel-ing of be - tray - al that I just can't seem to shake. And

ev -'ry-thing I know _ tells me that I should walk a - way, but I

just   want __ to   stay. ____   And my friends   say: __

𝄋 Chorus

I know you love her, but it's   o - ver, mate.   It does-n't mat - ter; put the

phone   a - way. _____   It's nev - er eas - y to walk a - way. Let her

Chorus

go, _____ it - 'll be o - kay.   It's gon-na hurt __ for a

bit of time, __   so bot-toms up, let's for - get   to - night. ____

To Coda ⊕

You'll find an - oth - er and you'll be   just   fine. __ Let her   go. _____

Bad Romance

Words and Music by Stefani Germanotta and Nadir Khayat

want your dis - ease. ____   I want your ev - 'ry - thing as
want your de - sign, ____   'cause you're a crim - i - nal as

long as it's free. ____ I want your love.
long as you're mine. ____ I want your love.

Love, love, love, I want your love.
Love, love, love, I want your love.

I want your dra - ma, the touch of your hand. ____
I want your psy - cho, your ver - ti - go shtick. ____

I want your leath - er - stud - ded kiss in the sand. __ I want your love.
Want you in my rear win - dow, ba - by, you're sick. __ I want your love.

Love, love, love, I want your love.)
Love, love, love, I want your love.)

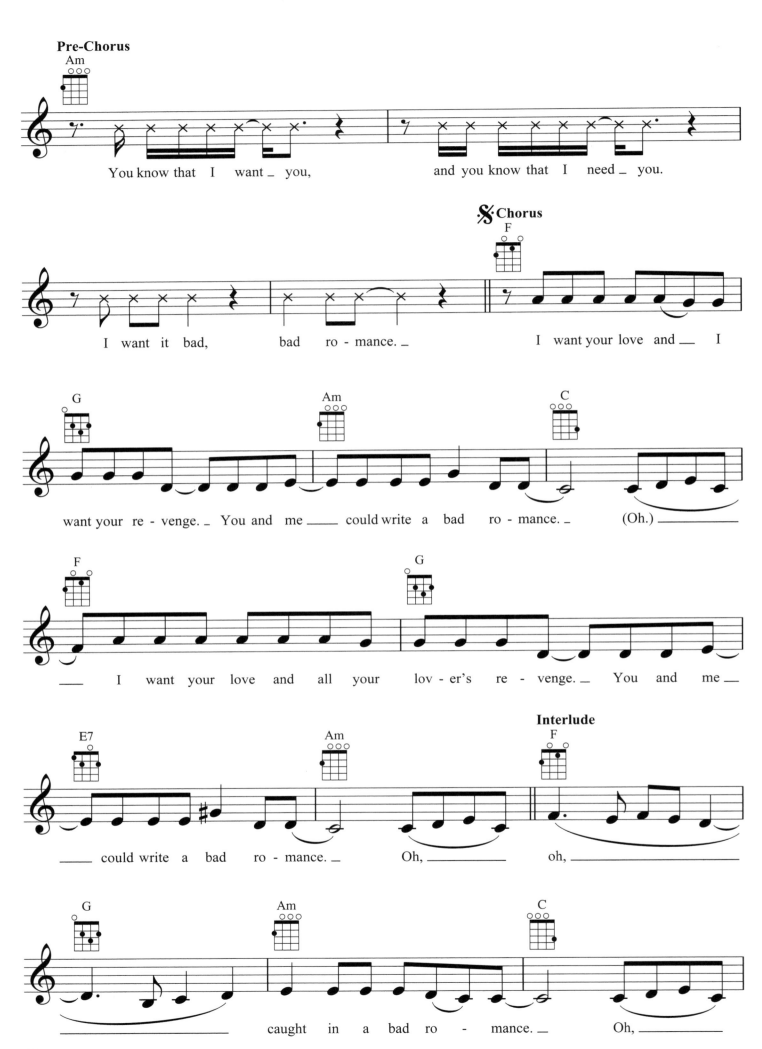

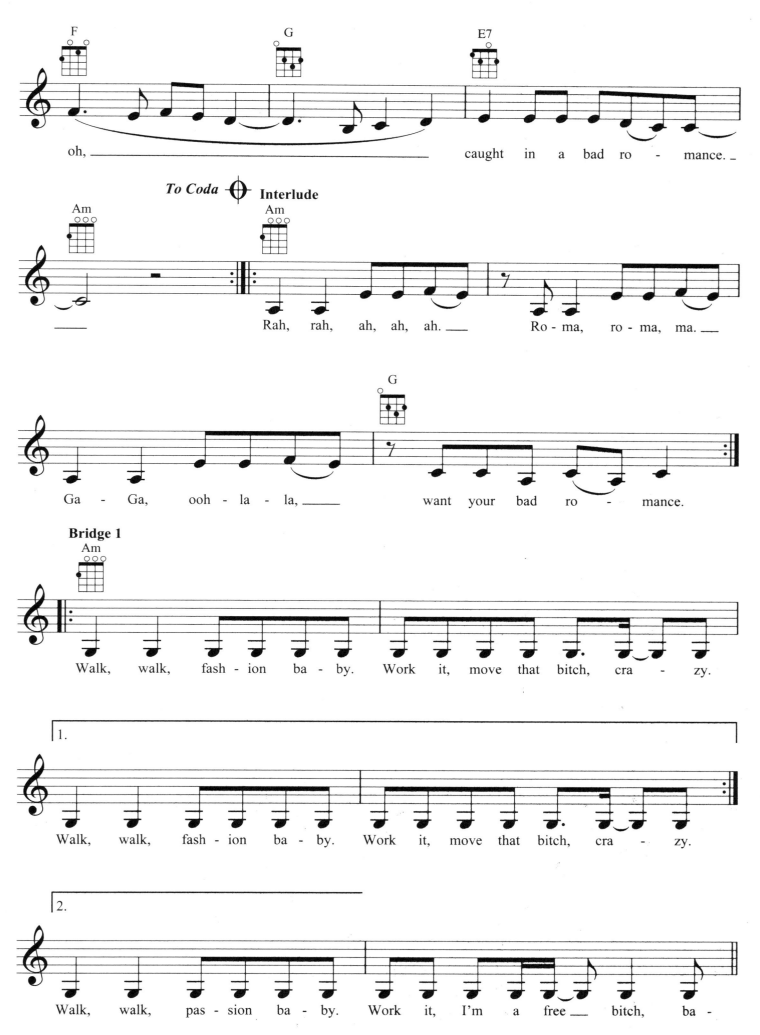

I don't wan - na be friends. _____

_____ (Oh, _____ oh, _____

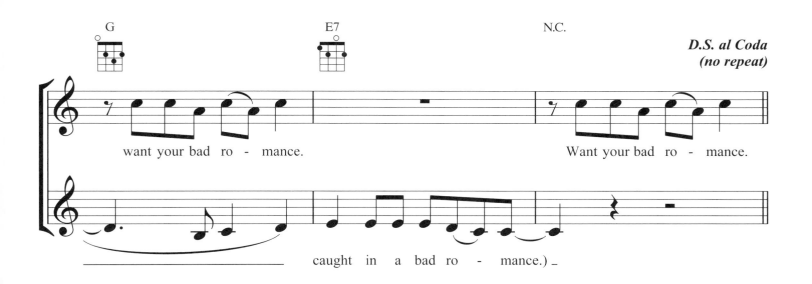

D.S. al Coda
(no repeat)

want your bad ro - mance. Want your bad ro - mance.

_____ caught in a bad ro - mance.) _

Coda
Outro
N.C.

Rah, rah, ah, ah, ah. _____ Ro - ma, ro - ma, ma. _____

Ga - Ga, ooh - la - la, _____ want your bad ro - mance.

Believer

Words and Music by Dan Reynolds, Wayne Sermon, Ben McKee, Daniel Platzman,
Justin Trantor, Mattias Larsson and Robin Fredricksson

1. First things first: I'm - a say all the words in - side my head. I'm fired up and tired of the way that things have been, oh, ooh, _____ the way that things have been, oh, ooh. _____

2. Sec - ond things sec - ond: don't you tell me what you think that I can be. I'm the one at the sail, I'm the mas - ter of my sea, oh, ooh, _____ the mas - ter of my sea, oh, ooh. _____

Pre-Chorus

I was bro - ken _____ from a young age, tak - ing my

sulk - ing ____ to the mass - es, writ - ing my po - ems ____ for the few that looked at me,

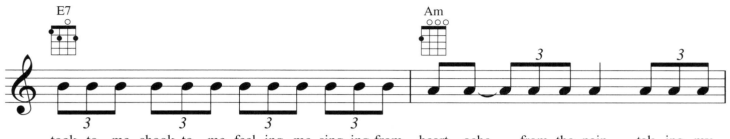

took to me, shook to me, feel - ing me sing - ing from heart - ache, ____ from the pain, tak - ing my

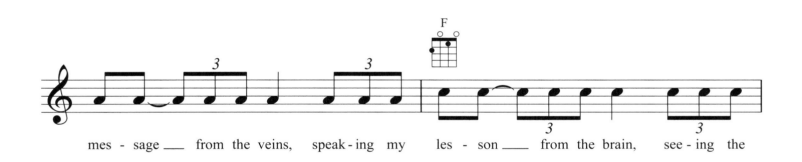

mes - sage ____ from the veins, speak - ing my les - son ____ from the brain, see - ing the

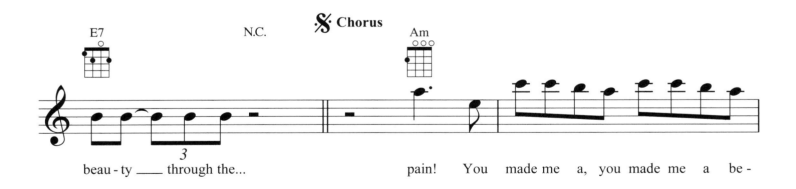

beau - ty ____ through the... pain! You made me a, you made me a be -

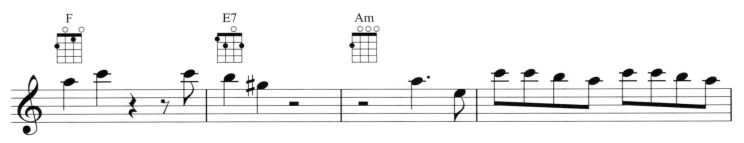

liev - er, be - liev - er. Pain! You break me down, you build me up; be -

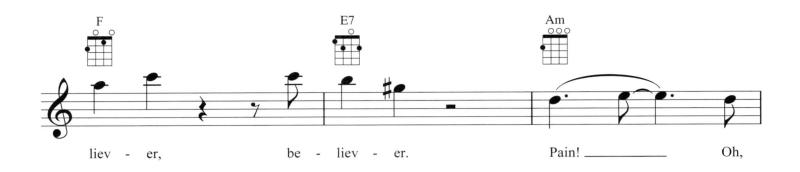

liev - er, be - liev - er. Pain! _____ Oh,

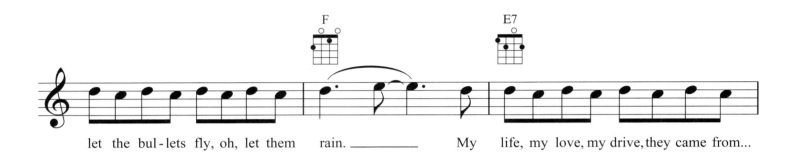

let the bul - lets fly, oh, let them rain. _____ My life, my love, my drive, they came from...

To Coda 1

To Coda 2

pain! You made me a, you made me a be - liev - er, be -

Verse

liev - er. 3. Third things third: send a prayer to the ones __ up a -

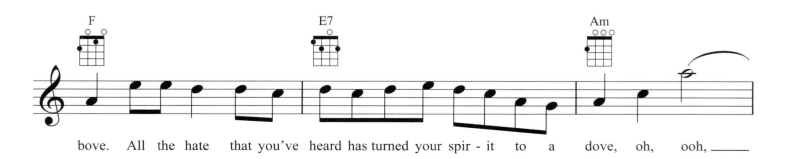

bove. All the hate that you've heard has turned your spir - it to a dove, oh, ooh, _____

your spir - it up a - bove, oh, ooh. _____ I was

Pre-Chorus

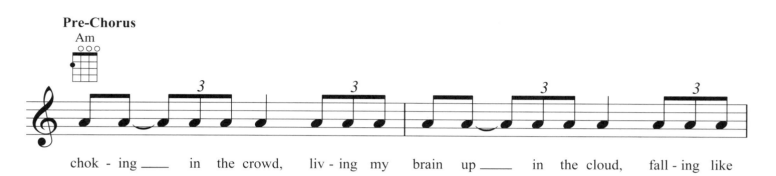

chok - ing _____ in the crowd, liv - ing my brain up _____ in the cloud, fall - ing like

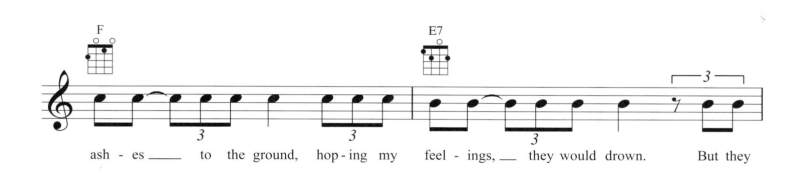

ash - es _____ to the ground, hop - ing my feel - ings, __ they would drown. But they

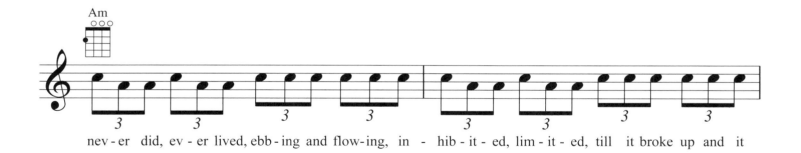

nev - er did, ev - er lived, ebb - ing and flow - ing, in - hib - it - ed, lim - it - ed, till it broke up and it

D.S. al Coda 1   **Coda 1**

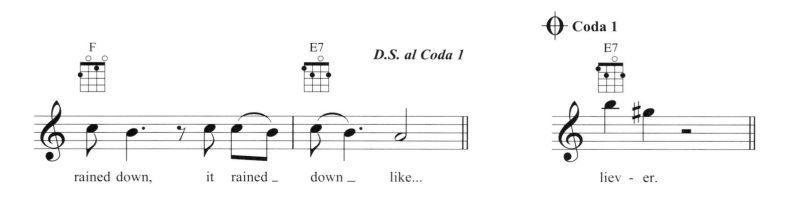

rained down, it rained __ down __ like...   liev - er.

Verse

4. Last things last: by the grace of the fi - re and the flames, you're the face of the

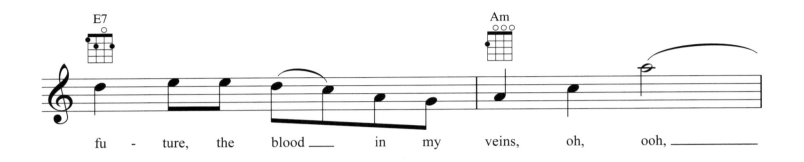

fu - ture, the blood ___ in my veins, oh, ooh, _____

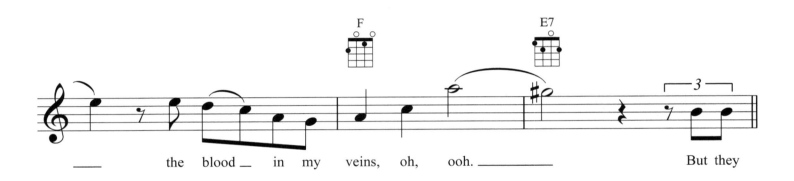

___ the blood _ in my veins, oh, ooh. _____ But they

Pre-Chorus

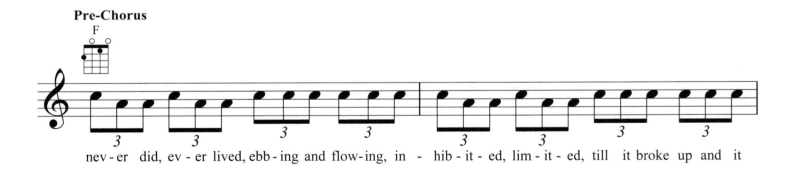

nev - er did, ev - er lived, ebb - ing and flow - ing, in - hib - it - ed, lim - it - ed, till it broke up and it

D.S. al Coda 2   Coda 2

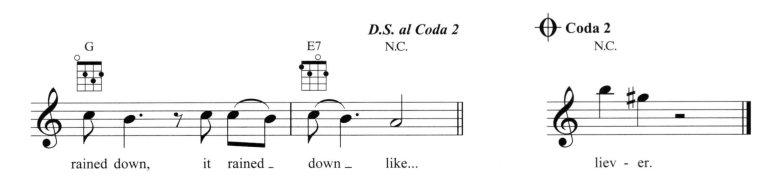

rained down, it rained _ down _ like...   liev - er.

Counting Stars

Words and Music by Ryan Tedder

Verse

life like a swing-in' vine, _____ swing my heart a-cross the line. __
(2.) *See additional lyrics*

In my face is flash-in' signs, _ seek it out and ye shall find. _

Old, but I'm not that old. Young, but I'm not that bold. And

I don't think the world is sold _ on just do-in' what we're told. _

Pre-Chorus

I, I _____ feel _ some-thin' so right do-in' the wrong _

_____ thing. _____ And I, I _____ feel _ some-thin' so

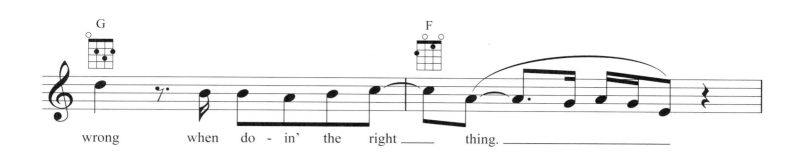

wrong   when   do - in'   the   right ___ thing. _____

I   could - n't   lie,   could - n't   lie,   could - n't   lie. ___   { Ev - 'ry - thing _ that
{ Ev - 'ry - thing _ that

𝄋 **Chorus**

N.C.

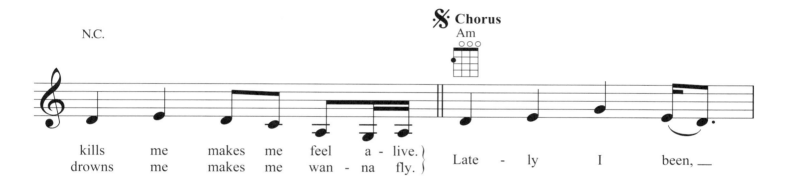

kills   me   makes   me   feel   a - live. }   Late - ly   I   been, ___
drowns   me   makes   me   wan - na   fly. }

I   been   los - in'   sleep ___   dream - in'   a - bout ___   the   things   that

we   could   be.   But,   ba - by,   I   been, _   I   been   pray - in'   hard. ___

Said   no   more   count - in'   dol - lars,   we'll   be   count - in'   stars.   Late - ly   I   been, ___

I been los-in' sleep __ dream-in' a-bout __ the things that

we could be. But, ba-by, I been, __ I been pray-in' hard. __

To Coda ⊕ | 1.

Said no more count-in' dol-lars, we'll be, we'll be count-in' stars. __

| 2.

2. I feel your stars. __

Bridge

N.C.(Am)

Oh. __ Take that mon-ey, watch __ it burn. __ Sink __

Play 4 times

__ in the riv-er the les-sons I've learned. Ev-'ry-thing __ that

kills   me   makes   me   feel   a - live.

Coda
Outro-Bridge

Take that mon - ey, watch __ it burn. __ Sink __ in the riv - er the les - sons I've learned.
stars. ____

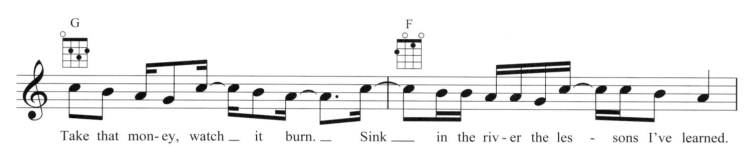

Take that mon - ey, watch __ it burn. __ Sink ___ in the riv - er the les - sons I've learned.

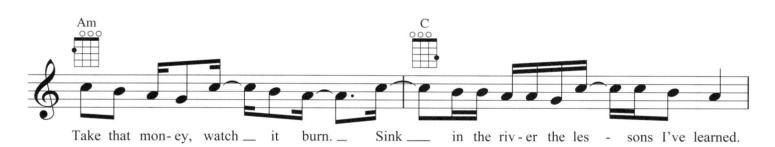

Take that mon - ey, watch __ it burn. __ Sink ___ in the riv - er the les - sons I've learned.

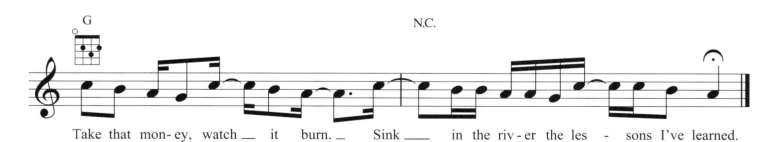

Take that mon - ey, watch __ it burn. __ Sink ___ in the riv - er the les - sons I've learned.

Additional Lyrics

2. I feel your love, and I feel it burn
   Down this river, every turn.
   Hope is a four-letter word.
   Make that money, watch it burn.

Best Day of My Life

Words and Music by Zachary Barnett, James Adam Shelley,
Matthew Sanchez, David Rublin, Shep Goodman and Aaron Accetta

First note

Verse
Happily

1. I had a dream so big and loud, I

jumped so high, I touched the clouds. _____ Whoa oh oh oh oh oh. _____

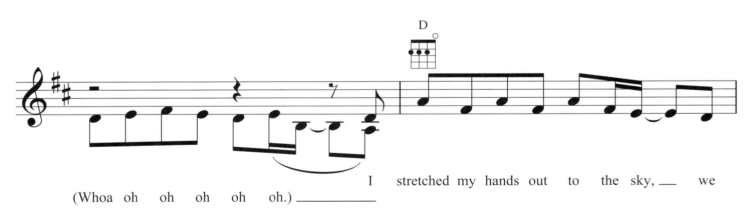

(Whoa oh oh oh oh oh.) _____ I stretched my hands out to the sky, _____ we

danced with mon-sters through the night. _____ Whoa oh oh oh oh oh. _____

Pre-Chorus

(Whoa oh oh oh oh oh.) _____ I'm nev-er gon-na look back, whoa.___ I'm

nev-er gon-na give it up, no._____ Please don't wake me now._____ (Two, three, four.)

Chorus

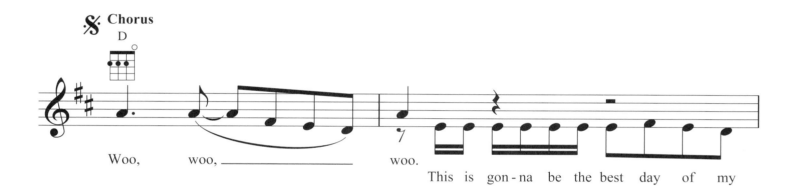

Woo, woo, _____ woo. This is gon-na be the best day of my

Woo, woo, _____ woo.

life._____ My li - i - i - i - i - ife._____

Woo, woo, _____ woo.

This is gon-na be the best day of my

Woo,   woo, _____ woo.
life. _____ My   li - i - i - i - i - ife. _____

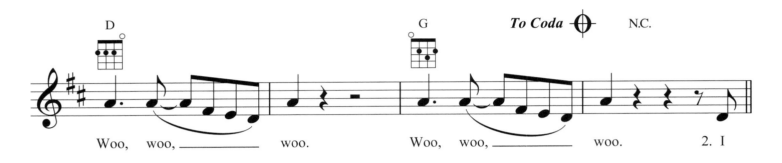

Woo,   woo, _____ woo.   Woo,   woo, _____ woo.   2. I

Verse

howled _ at   the   moon   with   friends _ and   then   the   sun   came   crash - ing   in. _____

Whoa   oh   oh   oh   oh   oh. _____
(Whoa   oh   oh   oh   oh   oh.) _____ But

all   the   pos - si - bil - i - ties, __ no   lim - its   just   e - piph - a - nies. _____

Whoa oh oh oh oh oh. _____ (Whoa oh oh oh oh oh.) _____ I'm

Pre-Chorus

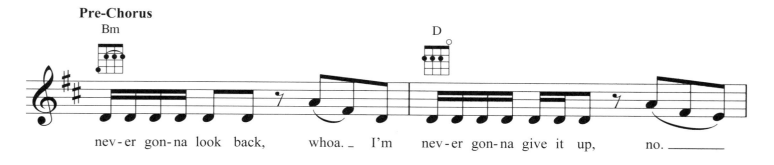

nev-er gon-na look back, whoa._ I'm nev-er gon-na give it up, no. _____

D.S. al Coda

⊕ **Coda**

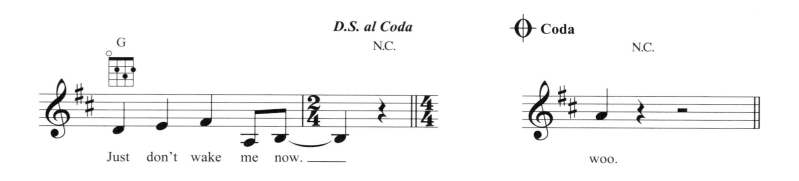

Just don't wake me now. _____

woo.

Bridge

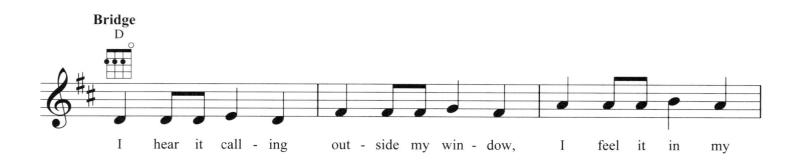

I hear it call-ing out-side my win-dow, I feel it in my

soul, _____ soul. _____ The stars are burn-ing so bright, the sun was out 'til mid-night.

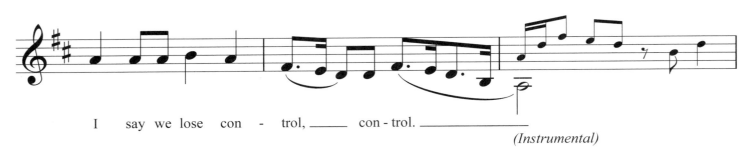

I say we lose con - trol, _____ con - trol. _____

(Instrumental)

Woo, woo, _____ woo.

Chorus

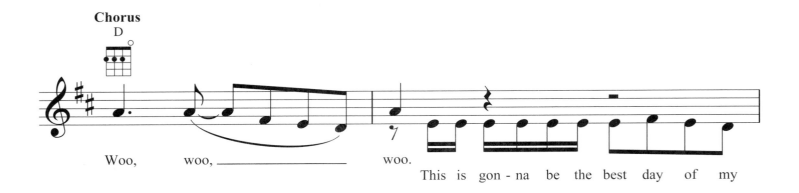

Woo, woo, _____ woo.

This is gon - na be the best day of my

Woo, woo, _____ woo.

life. _____ My li - i - i - i - i - ife. _____

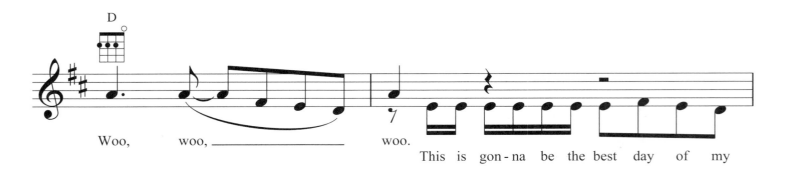

Woo, woo, _____ woo.

This is gon - na be the best day of my

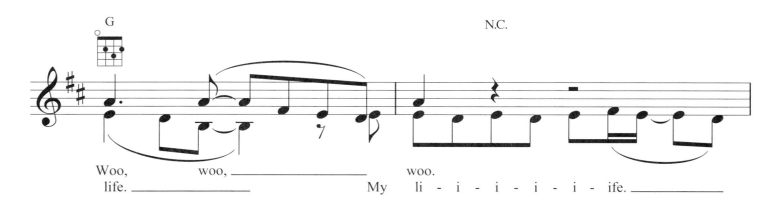

Woo,   woo, _____ woo.

life. _____   My   li - i - i - i - i - ife. _____

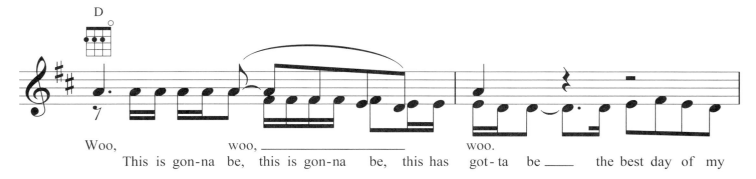

Woo,   woo, _____ woo.

This is gon-na be, this is gon-na be, this has got-ta be ____ the best day of my

Woo,   woo, _____ woo.

life. _____   Ev - 'ry-thing is look-ing up, ev-'ry-bod-y up now.

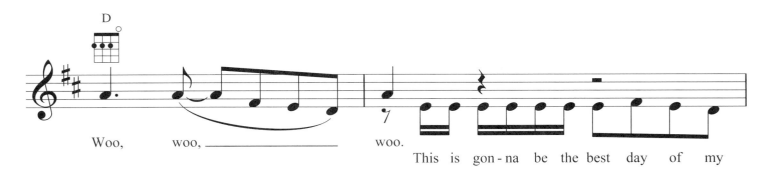

Woo,   woo, _____ woo.

This is gon-na be the best day of my

Woo,   woo, _____ woo.

life. _____   My   li - i - i - i - i - ife. _____

Broken

Words and Music by Mitchell Collins, Christian Medice and Samantha DeRosa

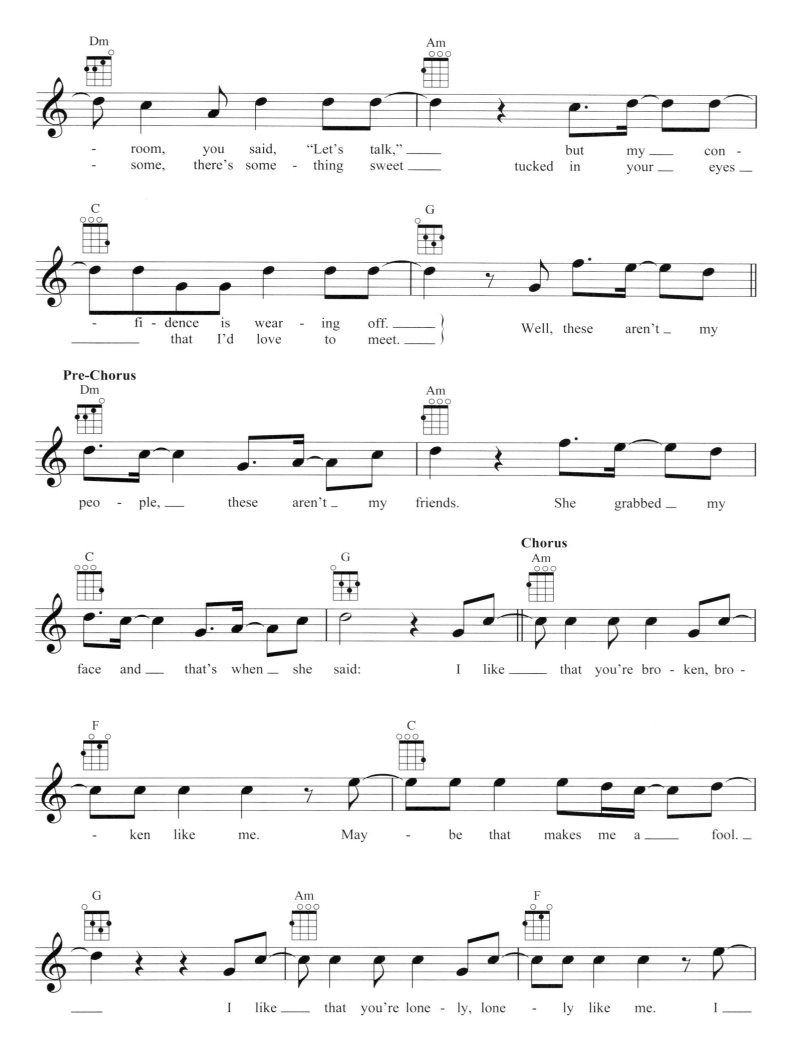

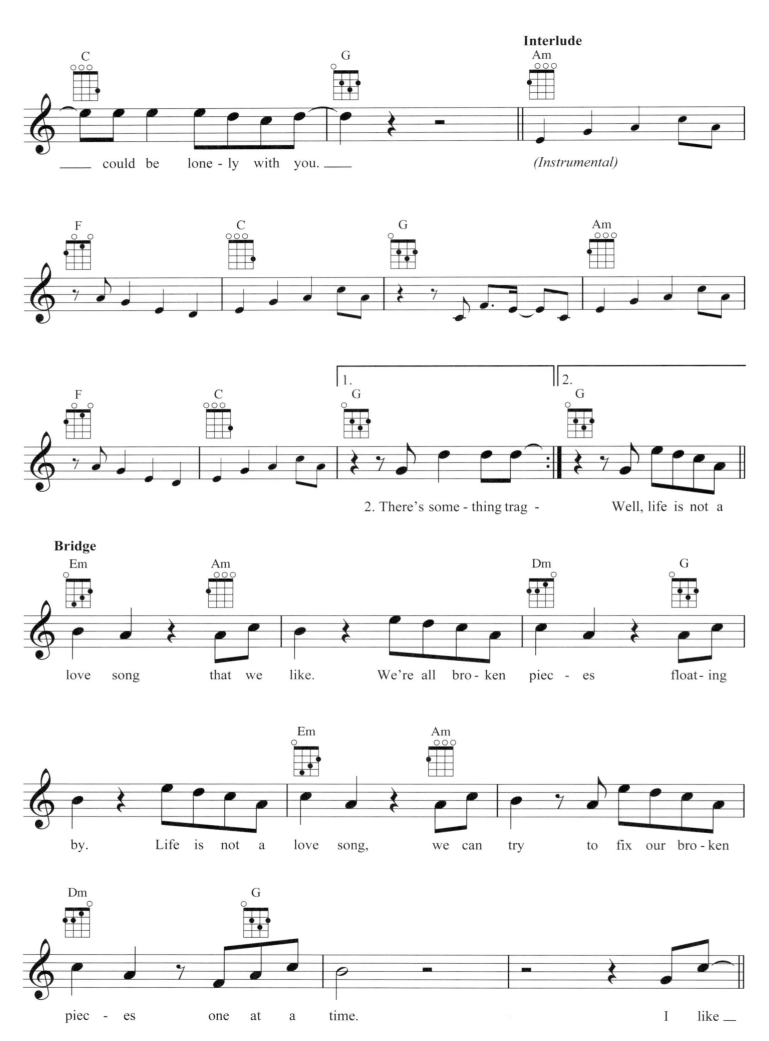

_____ could be lone - ly with you. _____

Interlude

(Instrumental)

1.   2.

2. There's some - thing trag -   Well, life is not a

Bridge

love song   that we like.   We're all bro - ken piec - es   float - ing

by.   Life is not a   love song,   we can   try   to fix our bro - ken

piec - es   one at a time.   I like _____

44

Budapest

Words and Music by George Barnett and Joel Pott

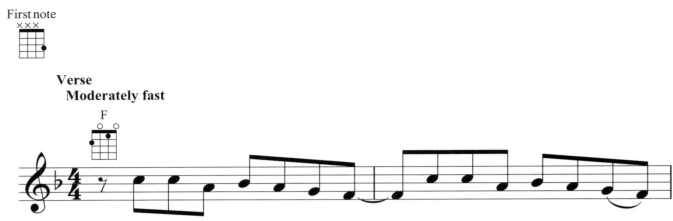

1. My house in Bu - da - pest; my, _____ my hid - den treas - ure chest; _

gold - en grand pi - an - o; _____ my beau - ti - ful cas - til - lo: you, ooh, _

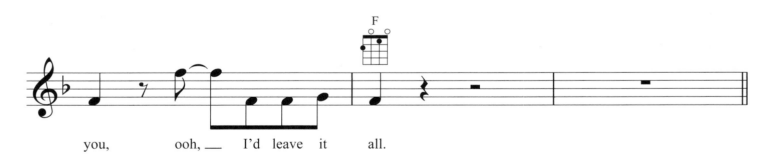

you, ooh, _ I'd leave it all.

2. My a - cres of a land _ I have a - chieved,
3. My man - y ar - ti - facts, _ the list goes on.
4. My friends and fam - i - ly, _____ they don't un - der - stand;

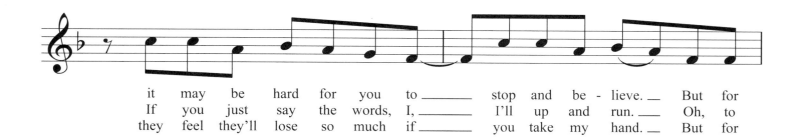

it may be hard for you to ___ stop and be - lieve. __ But for
If you just say the words, I, ___ I'll up and run. __ Oh, to
they feel they'll lose so much if ___ you take my hand. __ But for

you, ooh, __ you, ooh, __ I'd leave it all. Oh, for
you, ooh, __ you, ooh, __ I'd leave it all. Oh, to
you, ooh, __ you, ooh, __ I'd lose it all. Oh, for

you, ooh, __ you, ooh, __ I'd leave it all.
you, ooh, __ you, ooh, __ I'd leave it all.
you, ooh, __ you, ooh, __ I'd lose it all.

Chorus

Give me one good rea - son why I ___ should nev - er make a change. _

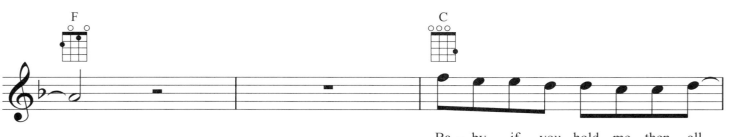

___ Ba - by, if you hold me then all __

_____ of this will go _____ a - way. _____

Chorus

Give me one good rea - son why I _____ should nev - er make a change. _

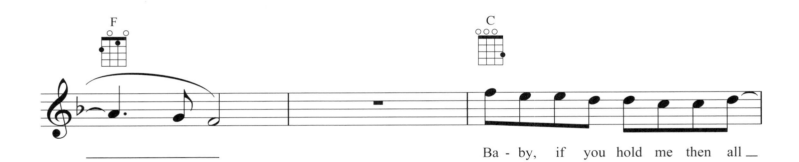

_____ Ba - by, if you hold me then all _

_____ of this will go _____ a - way. _____

Interlude

(Instrumental)

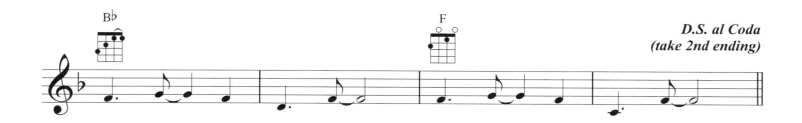

D.S. al Coda
(take 2nd ending)

Outro-Verse

Coda

My house in Bu - da - pest; my, ___ my hid - den treas - ure chest; ___

gold - en grand pi - an - o; _____ my beau - ti - ful cas - til - lo: you, ooh, ___

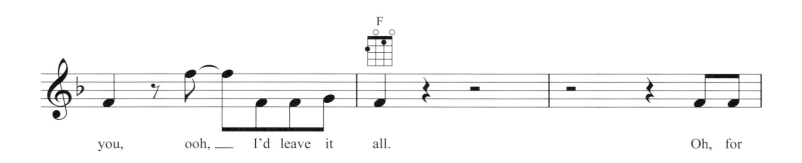

you, ooh, ___ I'd leave it all. Oh, for

you, ooh, ___ you, ooh, ___ I'd leave it all.

Cups
(When I'm Gone)

from the Motion Picture Soundtrack PITCH PERFECT
Words and Music by A.P. Carter, Luisa Gerstein and Heloise Tunstall-Behrens

miss me by my hair, ___ you'll miss me ev - 'ry - where. ___ Oh,
miss me by my walk, ___ you're gon - na miss me by my talk. ___ Oh,

you're gon - na miss ___ me when I'm gone. When I'm
you're gon - na miss ___ me when I'm gone. When I'm

gone, when I'm gone, _____ you're gon - na miss ___ me when I'm
gone, when I'm gone, _____ you're gon - na miss ___ me when I'm

gone. You're gon - na miss me by my walk, ___ you're gon - na
gone. You're gon - na miss me by my hair, ___ you're gon - na

To Coda ⊕

miss me by my talk. ___ Oh, ___ you're gon - na miss ___ me when I'm
miss me ev - 'ry - where. ___ Oh, ___ you're sure gon - na miss me when I'm

Verse

gone.   2. I got my tick - et for the long way ___ 'round,

Feel It Still

Words and Music by John Gourley, Zach Carothers, Jason Sechrist, Eric Howk, Kyle O'Quin,
Brian Holland, Freddie Gorman, Georgia Dobbins, Robert Bateman,
William Garrett, John Hill and Asa Taccone

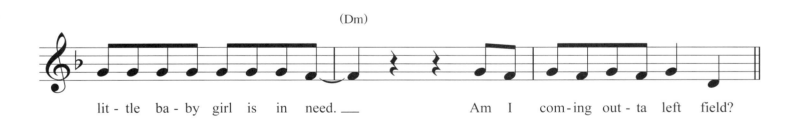

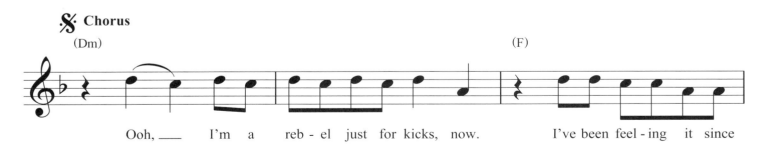

(Gm)

nine-teen six - ty - six, now.

{ Might be o - ver ___ now, but I feel it still. }
{ Might have had your _ fill, but you feel it still. }

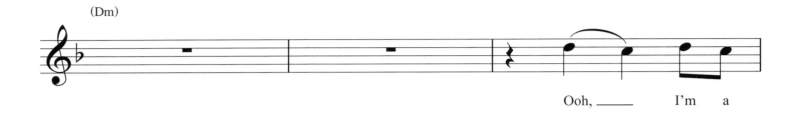

(Dm)

Ooh, _____ I'm a

(F)

reb - el just for kicks, now. Let me kick it like it's nine - teen eight - y - six, now.

To Coda ⊕

(Gm)

(Dm)

Might be o - ver ___ now, but I feel it still.

Verse
Dm

2. Got an - oth - er mouth to feed. _____

F

Gm

Leave it with a ba - by - sit - ter; Ma - ma, call the grave - dig - ger.

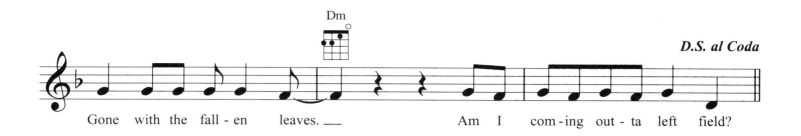

Gone with the fall - en leaves. ___ Am I com - ing out - ta left field?

Verse

Coda

3. We could fight a war for peace. ___ (Ooh, _____ I'm a

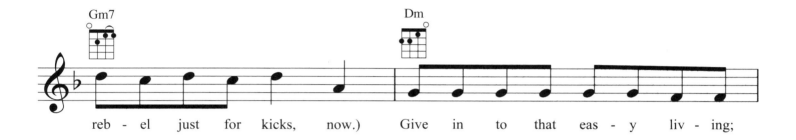

reb - el just for kicks, now.) Give in to that eas - y liv - ing;

good - bye to my hopes and dreams, ___ start

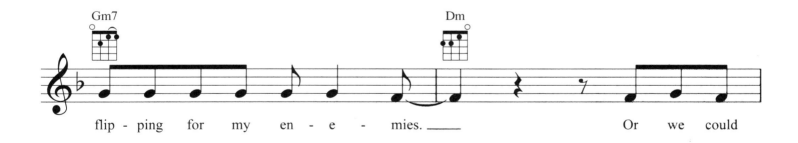

flip - ping for my en - e - mies. ___ Or we could

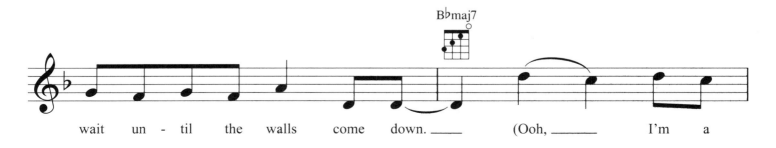

wait un - til the walls come down. ___ (Ooh, _____ I'm a

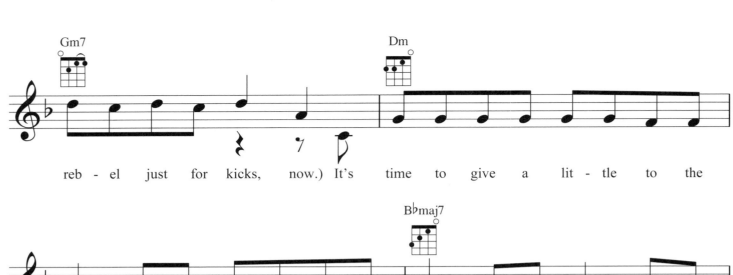

reb - el just for kicks, now.) It's time to give a lit - tle to the

kids in the mid - dle, but, oh, _____ un - til _____ it falls, _____

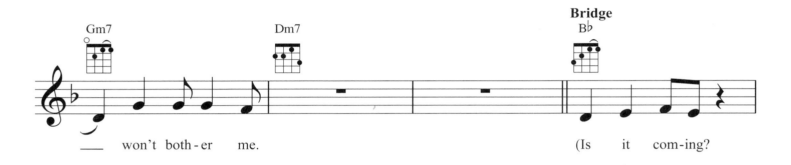

_____ won't both - er me. (Is it com - ing?

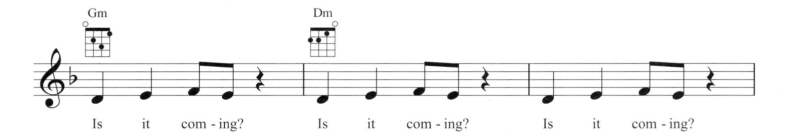

Is it com - ing? Is it com - ing? Is it com - ing?

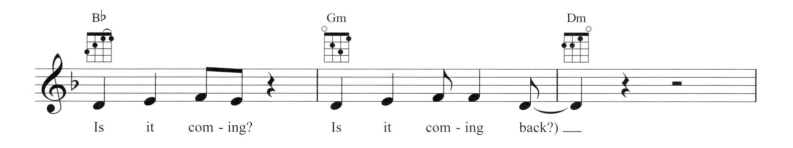

Is it com - ing? Is it com - ing back?) _____

Pre-Chorus

Ooh, _____ I'm a reb - el just for kicks. Yeah, your

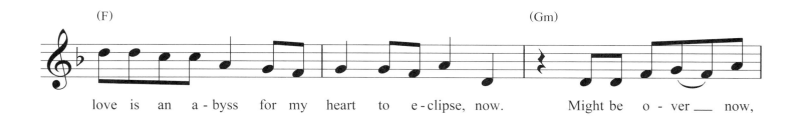

love is an a - byss for my heart to e - clipse, now.   Might be o - ver __ now,

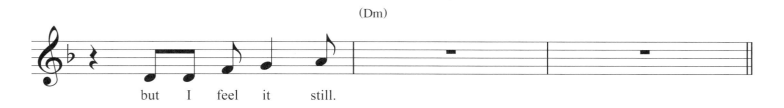

but I feel it still.

Chorus

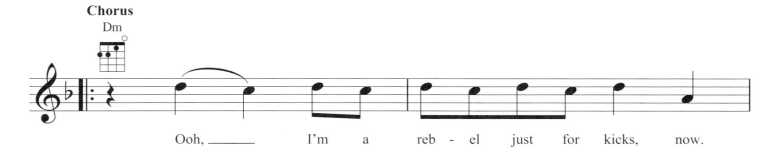

Ooh, _____ I'm a reb - el just for kicks, now.

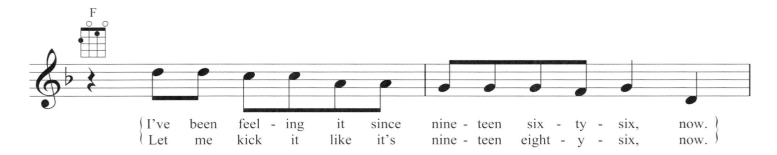

{ I've been feel - ing it since nine - teen six - ty - six, now. }
{ Let me kick it like it's nine - teen eight - y - six, now. }

1.

Might be o - ver __ now, but I feel it still.

2.

Might have had your fill, but you feel it still. ___

Despacito

Words and Music by Luis Fonsi, Erika Ender, Justin Bieber,
Jason Boyd, Marty James Garton and Ramón Ayala

First note

Verse
Moderate Latin beat, in 2

1. Come on o - ver in my di - rec - tion.

So thank - ful for that, it's such a bless - in', yeah.

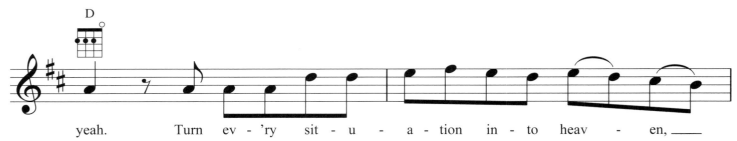

yeah. Turn ev - 'ry sit - u - a - tion in - to heav - en,

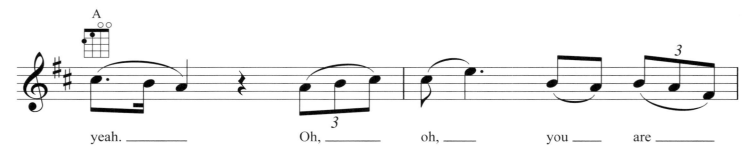

yeah. Oh, oh, you are my sun -

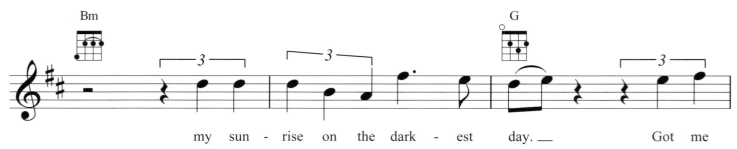

my sun - rise on the dark - est day. Got me

feel-in' some kind of way. ____ Make me wan-na sa-vor ev-'ry mo-ment slow-

-ly, slow-ly. _____ You fit me, tail-or-

made love, how you put it on. __ Got the on-ly key, know how to turn it on. __

The way you nib-ble on my ear, the on-ly words I wan-na hear: Ba-by, take it

Pre-Chorus

slow so we can last long. __ Tú, tú e-res el i-mán y yo soy el me-

tal. Me voy a-cer-can-do y voy ar-man-do el plan. Só-lo con pen-

sar - lo se a - ce - ler - a el pul - so. Oh, yeah.

Ya, ya me es - tá gus - tan - do más de lo nor - mal. To - dos mis sen -

ti - dos van pi - dien - do más. ____ Es - to hay que to - mar - lo sin nin - gún a - pu -

𝄋 Chorus 1

- ro. Des - pa - ci - to. Quie - ro res - pi -

rar tu cue - llo des - pa - ci - to. De - ja que te di - ga co - sas al o - í -

- do, pa - ra que te a - cuer - des si no es - tás con - mi - go.

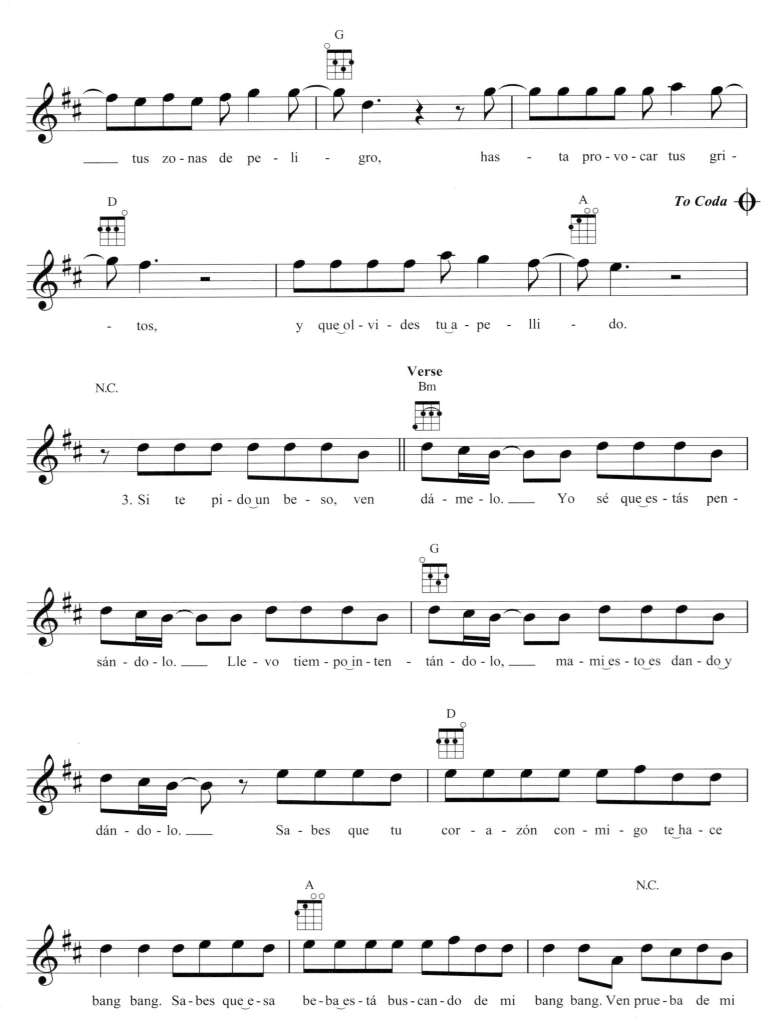

_____ tus zo - nas de pe - li - gro, has - ta pro-vo-car tus gri -

To Coda

- tos, y que ol - vi - des tu a - pe - lli - do.

Verse

3. Si te pi - do un be - so, ven dá - me - lo. _____ Yo sé que es - tás pen -

sán - do - lo. _____ Lle - vo tiem - po in - ten - tán - do - lo, _____ ma - mi es - to es dan - do y

dán - do - lo. _____ Sa - bes que tu cor - a - zón con - mi - go te ha - ce

bang bang. Sa - bes que e - sa be - ba es - tá bus - can - do de mi bang bang. Ven prue - ba de mi

bo - ca pa - ra ver có - mo te sa - be. Quie - ro, quie - ro, quie - ro ver cuán - to a - mor a ti te

ca - be. Yo no ten - go pri - sa, yo me quie - ro dar el via - je. Em - pe - ce - mos

Bridge

len - to, des - pués sal - va - je. Pa - si - to a pa - si - to, sua - ve sua - ve -

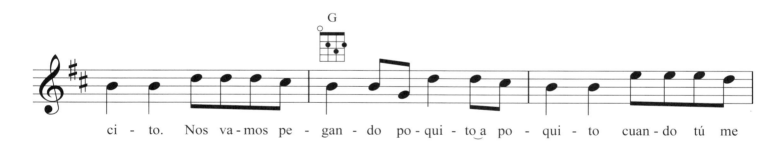

ci - to. Nos va - mos pe - gan - do po - qui - to a po - qui - to cuan - do tú me

be - sas con e - sa de - stre - za. Veo que e - res ma - li - cia con ___ de - li - ca -

de - za. Pa - si - to a pa - si - to, sua - ve sua - ve - ci - to. Nos va - mos pe -

gan - do po - qui - to a po - qui - to. Y es que e - sa be - lle - za en un rom - pe - ca -

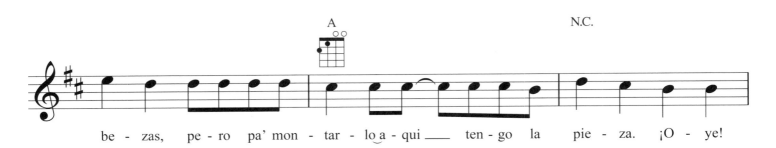

be - zas, pe - ro pa' mon - tar - lo a - qui ___ ten - go la pie - za. ¡O - ye!

Coda

D.S. al Coda

Chorus 2

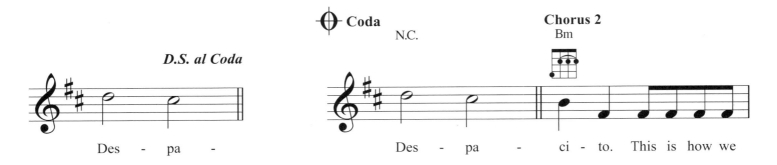

Des - pa -   Des - pa - ci - to. This is how we

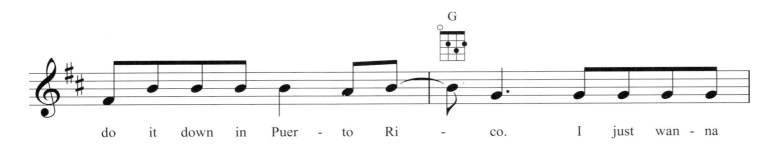

do it down in Puer - to Ri - co. I just wan - na

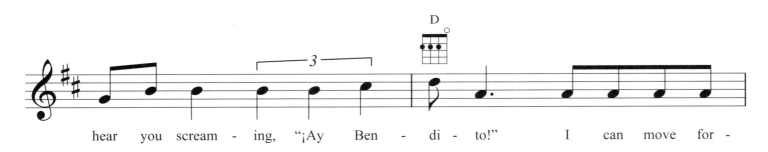

hear you scream - ing, "¡Ay Ben - di - to!" I can move for -

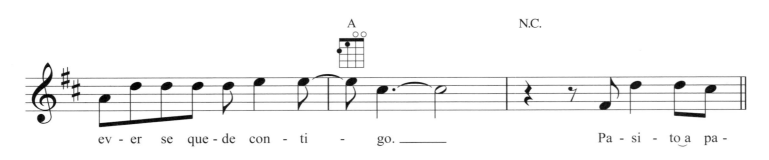

ev - er se que - de con - ti - go. ___   Pa - si - to a pa -

Outro-Bridge

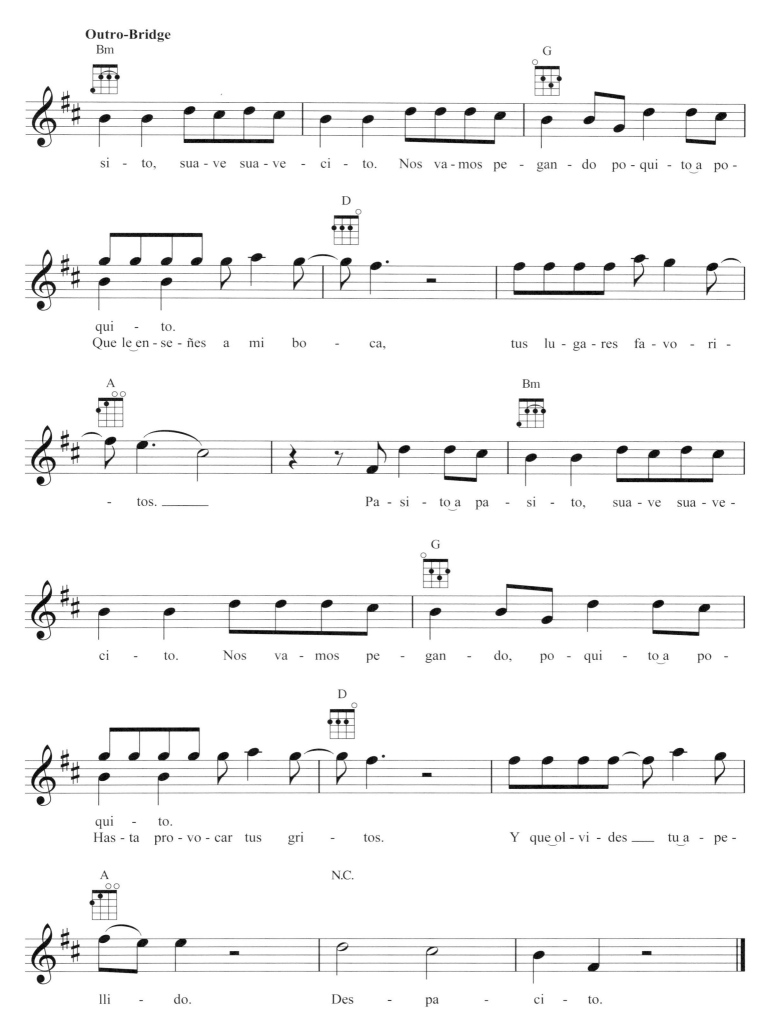

si - to, sua - ve sua - ve - ci - to. Nos va - mos pe - gan - do po - qui - to a po -

qui - to.
Que le en - se - ñes a mi bo - ca, tus lu - ga - res fa - vo - ri -

- tos. _____ Pa - si - to a pa - si - to, sua - ve sua - ve -

ci - to. Nos va - mos pe - gan - do, po - qui - to a po -

qui - to.
Has - ta pro - vo - car tus gri - tos. Y que ol - vi - des ___ tu a - pe -

lli - do. Des - pa - ci - to.

Get Lucky

**Words and Music by Thomas Bangalter, Guy Manuel Homem Christo,
Nile Rodgers and Pharrell Williams**

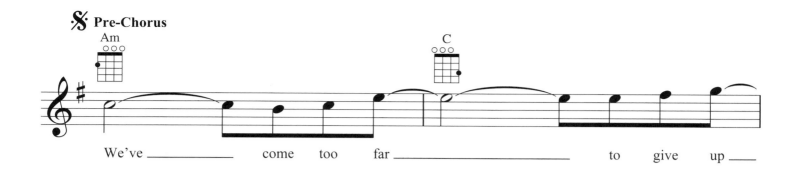

We've _____ come too far _____ to give up ____

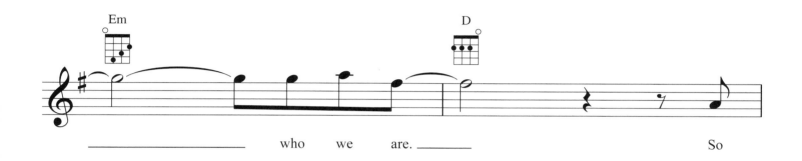

_____ who we are. _____ So

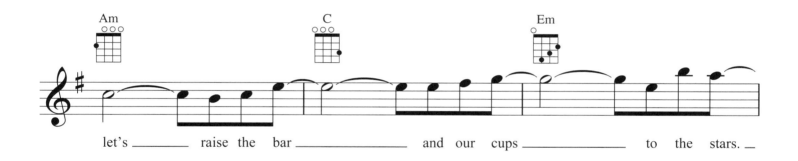

let's _____ raise the bar _____ and our cups _____ to the stars. __

Chorus

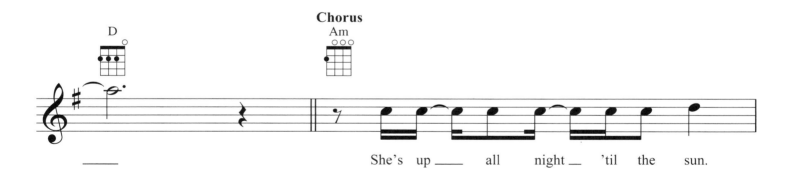

____ She's up ____ all night __ 'til the sun.

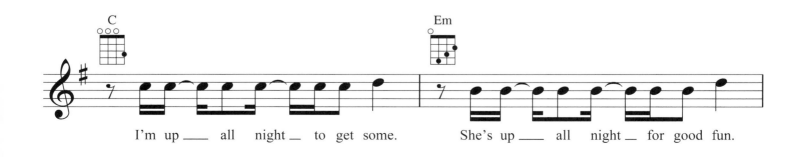

I'm up __ all night __ to get some. She's up __ all night __ for good fun.

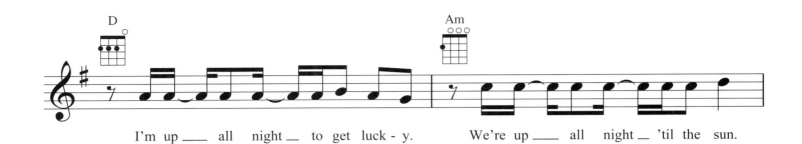

I'm up ___ all night ___ to get luck - y.
We're up ___ all night ___ 'til the sun.

We're up ___ all night ___ to get some.
We're up ___ all night ___ for good fun.

We're up ___ all night ___ to get luck - y.
We're up ___ all night ___ to get luck - y.

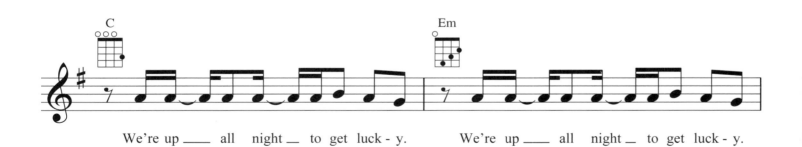

We're up ___ all night ___ to get luck - y.
We're up ___ all night ___ to get luck - y.

We're up ___ all night ___ to get luck - y.
We're up ___ all night ___ to get luck - y.

We're up ___ all night ___ to get luck - y. We're up ___ all night ___ to get luck - y.

2nd time, D.S. al Coda
(take 2nd ending)

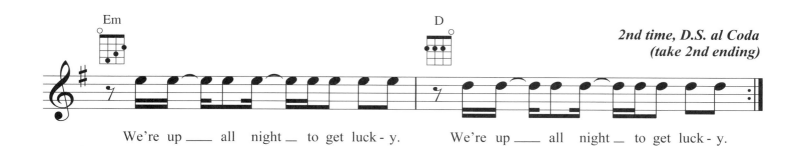

We're up ___ all night ___ to get luck - y. We're up ___ all night ___ to get luck - y.

Coda
Outro

We're up ___ all night ___ to get luck - y.

We're up ___ all night ___ to get luck - y. We're up ___ all night ___ to get luck - y.

We're up ___ all night ___ to get luck - y.

Happier

Words and Music by Marshmello, Steve Mac and Dan Smith

think that we both know the way that the sto - ry ___ ends. }
least we can swim far a - way from the wreck we ___ made. }

Then,

Pre-Chorus

on - ly for a min - ute, I want to change my mind 'cause this just don't feel

right to me. I want to raise your spir - its, I want to see you

smile, but know that means I'll have to leave. *(Instrumental)*

Know that means I'll have to leave.

Chorus

Late - ly, I've been, I've been think - ing I want you to be

like this, I think that you'll be hap-pi-er, I want you to be

Pre-Chorus

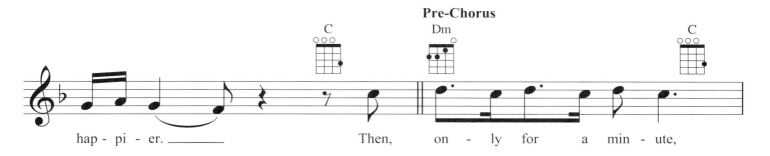

hap-pi-er. _____ Then, on-ly for a min-ute,

I want to change my mind 'cause this just don't feel right to me. I

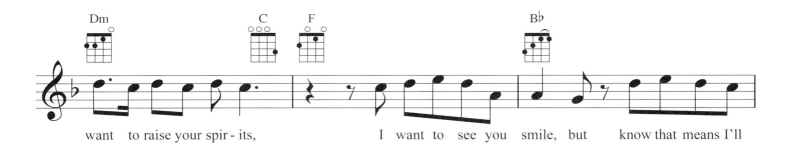

want to raise your spir-its, I want to see you smile, but know that means I'll

Outro

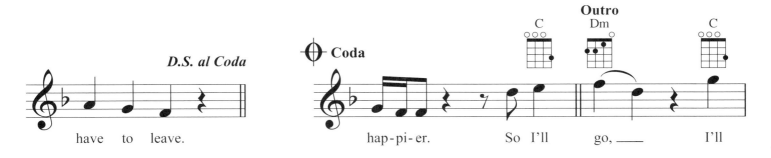

D.S. al Coda

Coda

have to leave. hap-pi-er. So I'll go, ____ I'll

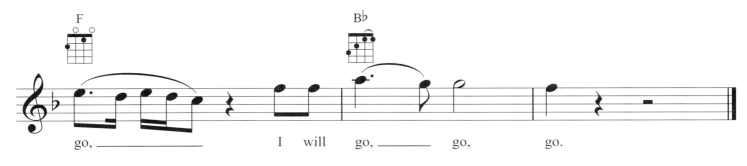

go, _____ I will go, _____ go, go.

Happy

from DESPICABLE ME 2

Words and Music by Pharrell Williams

like I don't care, _____ ba-by, by the way. _____

No of-fense to you, _____ don't waste your time.

_____ Here's why: Huh! } (Be-cause I'm hap-py.) Clap a-long if _____

Chorus

_____ you feel like a room with-out a roof. _____ (Be-cause I'm

hap-py.) Clap a-long if _____ you feel _____ like hap-pi-ness is the truth. _____

_____ (Be-cause I'm hap-py.) Clap a-long _____ if _____ you know what

hap-pi-ness is to you. _____ (Be-cause I'm hap-py.) Clap a-long if _____

you feel ___ like that's what you wan - na do. ___

Bridge

N.C.(A7)

Bring me down, _____ can't noth - in' bring me down; _

_____ your love is too high. Bring me down, _____ can't noth - in'

1.

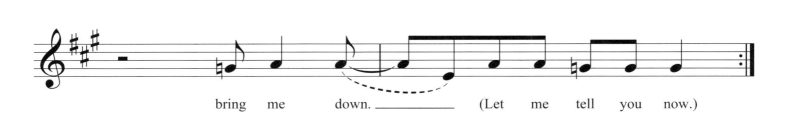

bring me down. _____ (Let me tell you now.)

Chorus

2., 3.   Fmaj7

___ I said... (Be - cause I'm hap - py.) Clap a - long if ___

Em7   A7

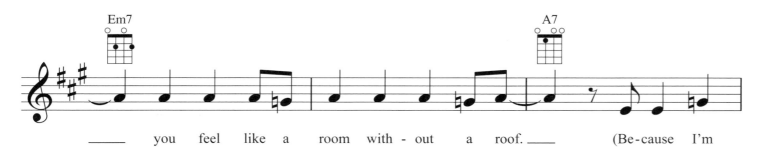

_____ you feel like a room with - out a roof. ___ (Be-cause I'm

Havana

Words and Music by Camila Cabello, Louis Bell, Pharrell Williams, Adam Feeney, Ali Tamposi, Jeffery Lamar Williams, Brian Lee, Andrew Wotman, Brittany Hazzard and Kaan Gunesberk

And then I had to tell him I had to go, __ oh, na na na na na. Ha-

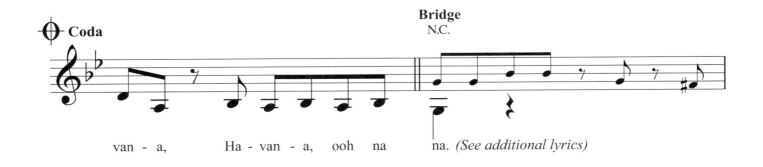

van - a, Ha - van - a, ooh na na. *(See additional lyrics)*

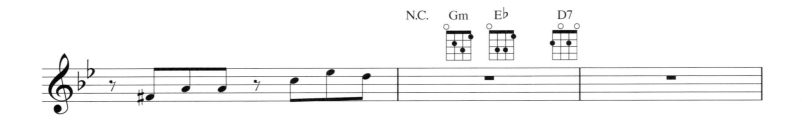

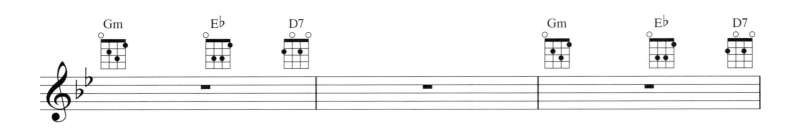

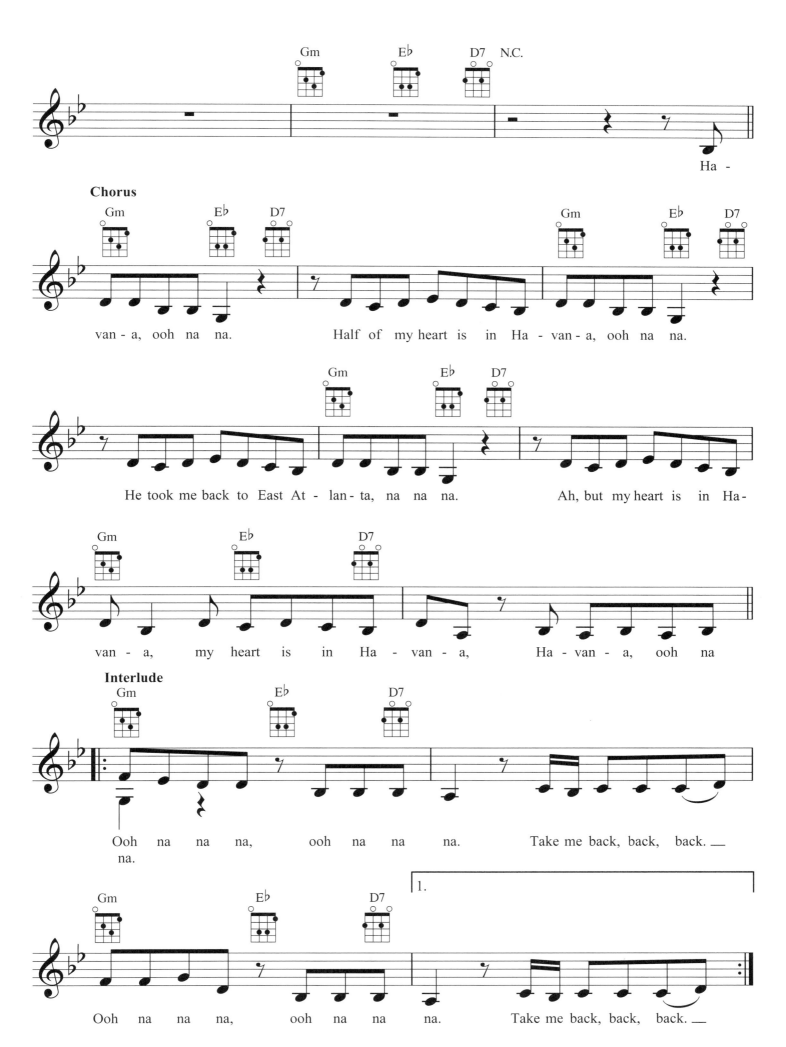

Outro

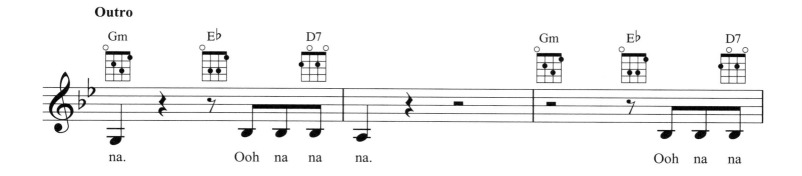

na.   Ooh na na na.   Ooh na na

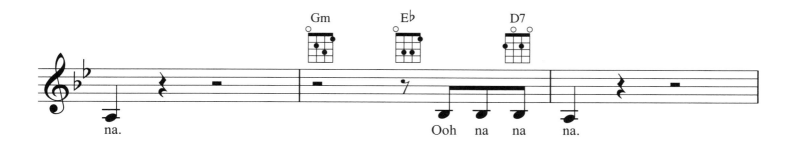

na.   Ooh na na na.

Ooh na na na.   Ha - van - a, ooh na na.

Additional Lyrics

Jeffery,
Just graduated, fresh on campus, mmm.
Fresh out East Atlanta with no manners, damn.
Fresh out East Atlanta.
Bump on her bumper like a traffic jam (jam).
Hey, I was quick to pay that girl like Uncle Sam. (Here you go, ay).
Back it on me, shawty cravin' on me.
Get to diggin' on me (on me).
She waited on me. (Then what?)
Shawty cakin' on me, got the bacon on me. (Wait up.)
This is history in the makin' on me (on me).
Point blank, close range, that be.
If it cost a million, that's me (that's me).
I was gettin' moola, man, they feel me.

Hello

Words and Music by Adele Adkins and Greg Kurstin

First note

Verse
Moderately

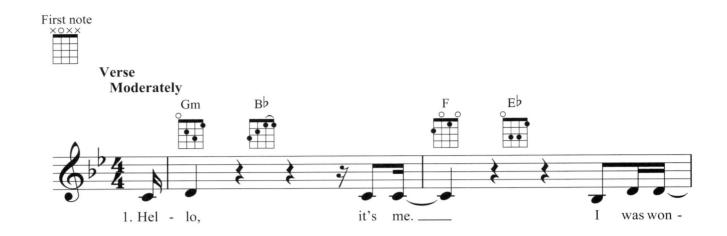

1. Hel - lo, it's me. ___ I was won -

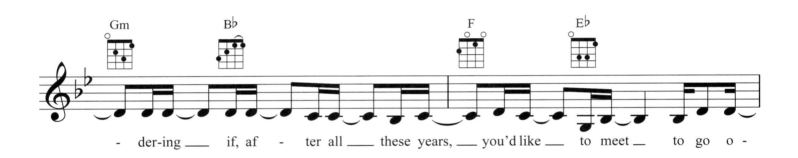

- der-ing ___ if, af - ter all ___ these years, ___ you'd like ___ to meet ___ to go o -

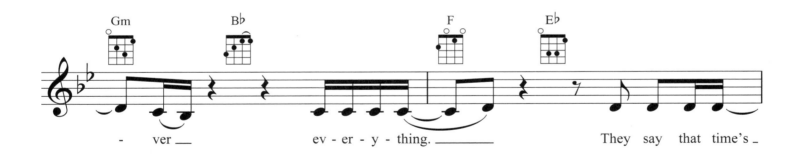

- ver ___ ev - er - y - thing. ___ They say that time's ___

___ sup-posed ___ to heal ___ ya, ___ but I ain't done much ___ heal - ing. 2. Hel -

Verse

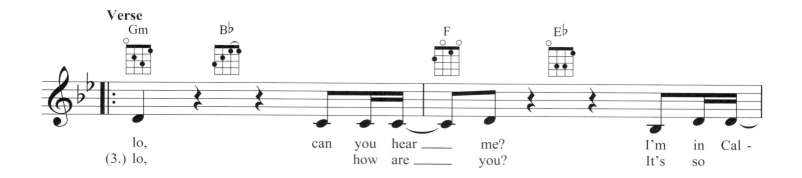

lo,   can you hear ___ me?   I'm in Cal -
(3.) lo,   how are ___ you?   It's so

- i-for - nia dream - ing a - bout who ___ we used ___ to be ___ when we were young -
typ - i-cal ___ of me ___ to talk ___ a - bout ___ my-self; ___ I'm sor - ry. I hope _

- er ___   and   free. _____   I've for - got -
___   that you're well. ___   Did you ev -

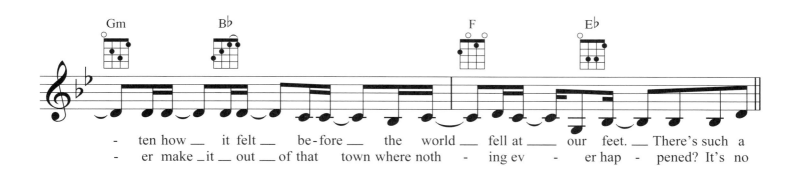

- ten how ___ it felt ___ be-fore ___ the world ___ fell at ___ our feet. There's such a
- er make _ it _ out _ of that town where noth - ing ev - er hap - pened? It's no

Pre-Chorus

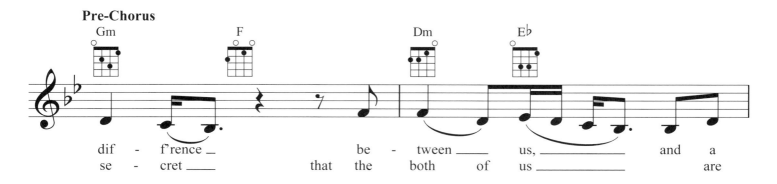

dif - f'rence _   be - tween _____ us, _____ and a
se - cret ___   that the both of us _____ are

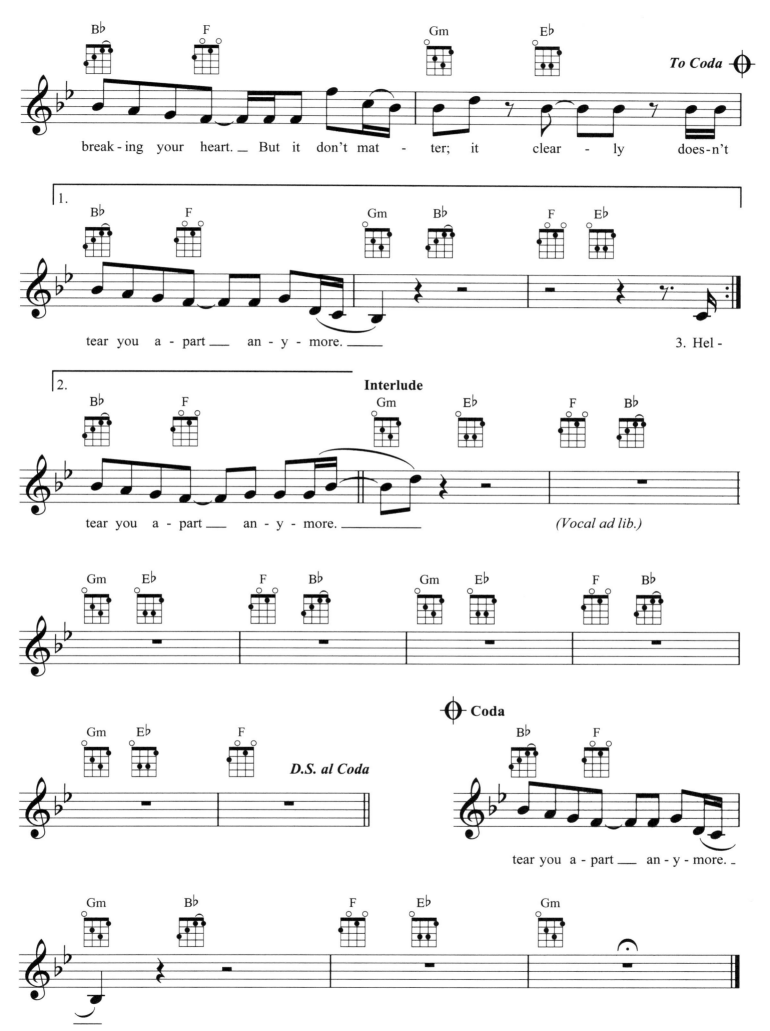

Hey, Soul Sister

Words and Music by Pat Monahan, Espen Lind and Amund Bjorklund

* Originally recorded in E major.

Chorus

89

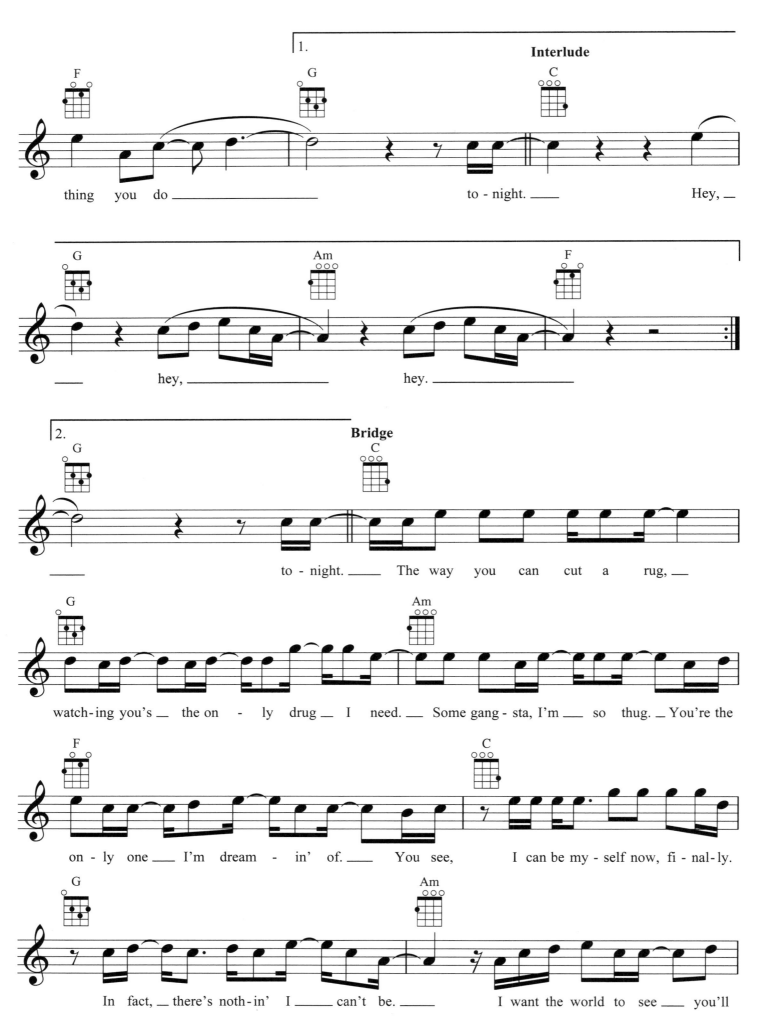

Additional Lyrics

2. Just in time, I'm so glad you have a one-track mind like me.
    You gave my life direction,
    A game-show love connection we can't deny.
    I'm so obsessed, my heart is bound to beat right out my untrimmed chest.
    I believe in you. Like a virgin, you're Madonna
    And I'm always gonna wanna blow your mind.

High Hopes

Words and Music by Brendon Urie, Samuel Hollander, William Lobban Bean, Jonas Jeberg, Jacob Sinclair, Jenny Owen Youngs, Ilsey Juber, Lauren Pritchard and Tayla Parx

"Ful-fill the proph-e-cy. Be some-thing great. __ Go make a leg-a-cy."

Man-i-fest des-ti-ny. Back in the days, __ we want-ed ev-'ry-thing, want-ed

ev-'ry-thing. Ma-ma said, "Burn your bi-o-graph-ies.

Re-write your his-to-ry. Light up your wild-est dreams." Mu-se-um vic-to-ries,

ev-er-y day. __ We want-ed ev-'ry-thing, want-ed ev-'ry-thing. Ma-ma said, __

Pre-Chorus

___ "Don't give up. ___ It's a lit - tle com - pli-cat-

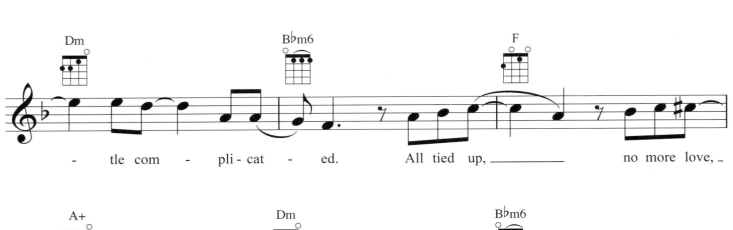

- tle com - pli - cat - ed. All tied up, _____ no more love, _

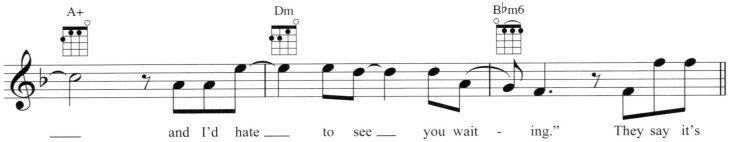

_____ and I'd hate ___ to see ___ you wait - ing." They say it's

Bridge 2

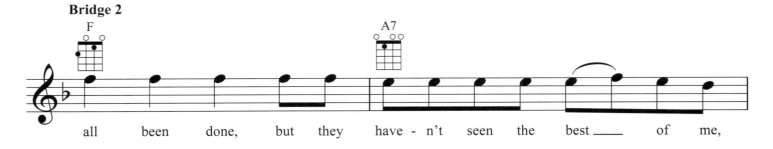

all been done, but they have - n't seen the best ___ of me,

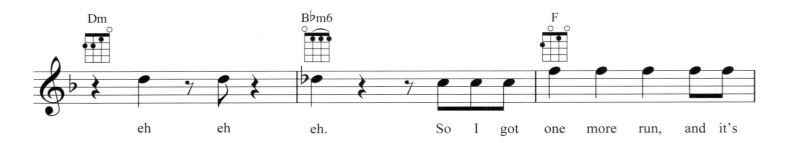

eh eh eh. So I got one more run, and it's

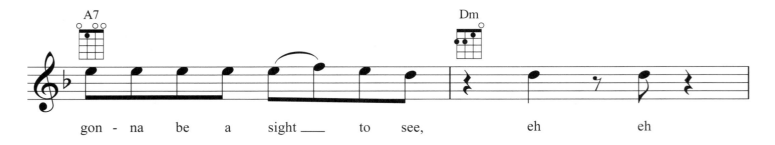

gon - na be a sight ___ to see, eh eh

D.S. al Coda
(with repeat)

Coda

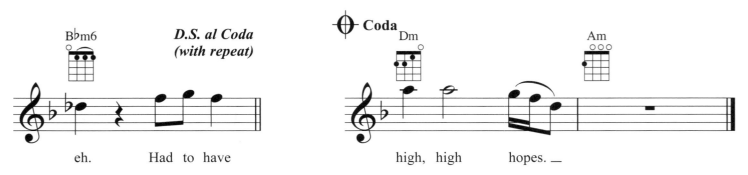

eh. Had to have high, high hopes. _

Heaven

Words and Music by Shy Carter, Lindsay Rimes and Matthew McGinn

Ev-'ry-bod-y's talk-in' 'bout heav-en like they just can't wait to go, ___

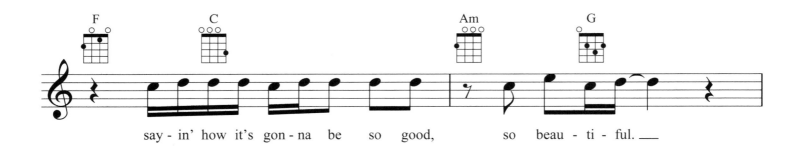

say-in' how it's gon-na be so good, so beau-ti-ful. ___

Ly-in' next to you, ___ in this bed with you, ___ I ain't con-vinced. ___ 'Cause

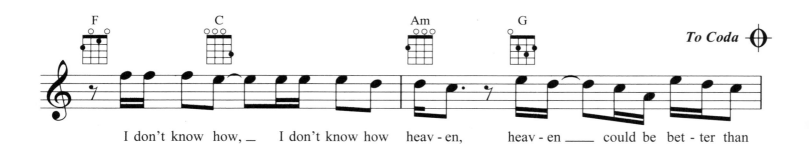

I don't know how, ___ I don't know how heav-en, heav-en ___ could be bet-ter than

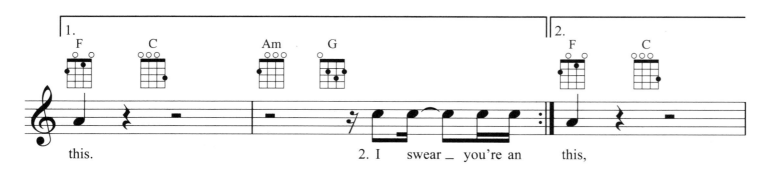

this.   2. I swear ___ you're an   this,

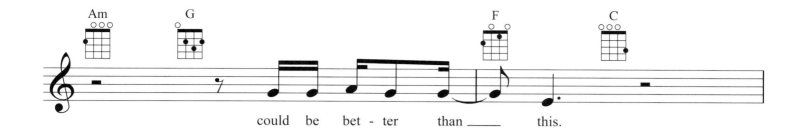
could be bet - ter than _____ this.

D.S. al Coda

⊕ **Coda**

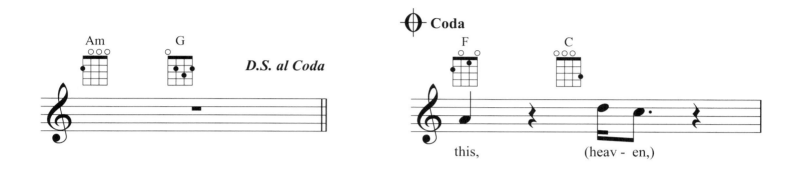
this, (heav - en,)

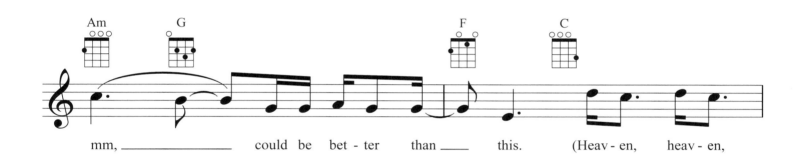
mm, _____ could be bet - ter than _____ this. (Heav - en, heav - en,

Outro

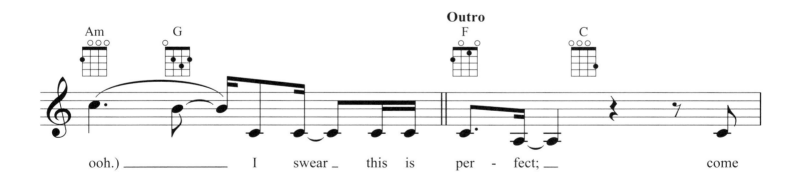
ooh.) _____ I swear _ this is per - fect; _ come

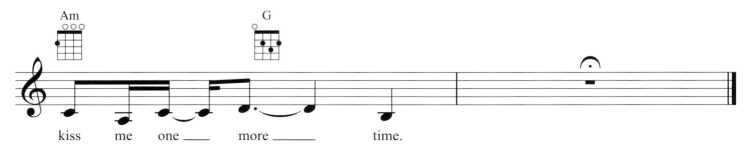
kiss me one _____ more _____ time.

Ho Hey

Words and Music by Jeremy Fraites and Wesley Schultz

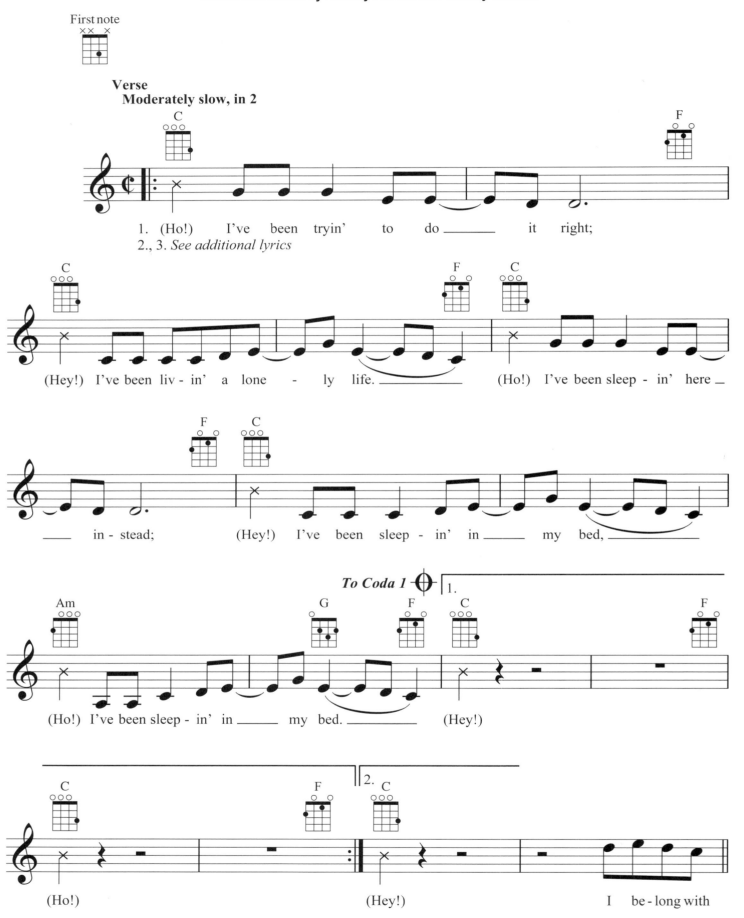

Additional Lyrics

2. (Ho!) So show me, family,
   (Hey!) All the blood that I will bleed.
   (Ho!) I don't know where I belong,
   (Hey!) I don't know where I went wrong,
   (Ho!) But I can write a song.
   (Hey!)

3. (Ho!) I don't think you're right for him.
   (Hey!) Look at what it might have been if you
   (Ho!) Took a bus to Chinatown.
   (Hey!) I'd be standing on Canal
   (Ho!) And Bowery. *(To Coda 1)*

I Don't Know My Name

Words and Music by Grace VanderWaal

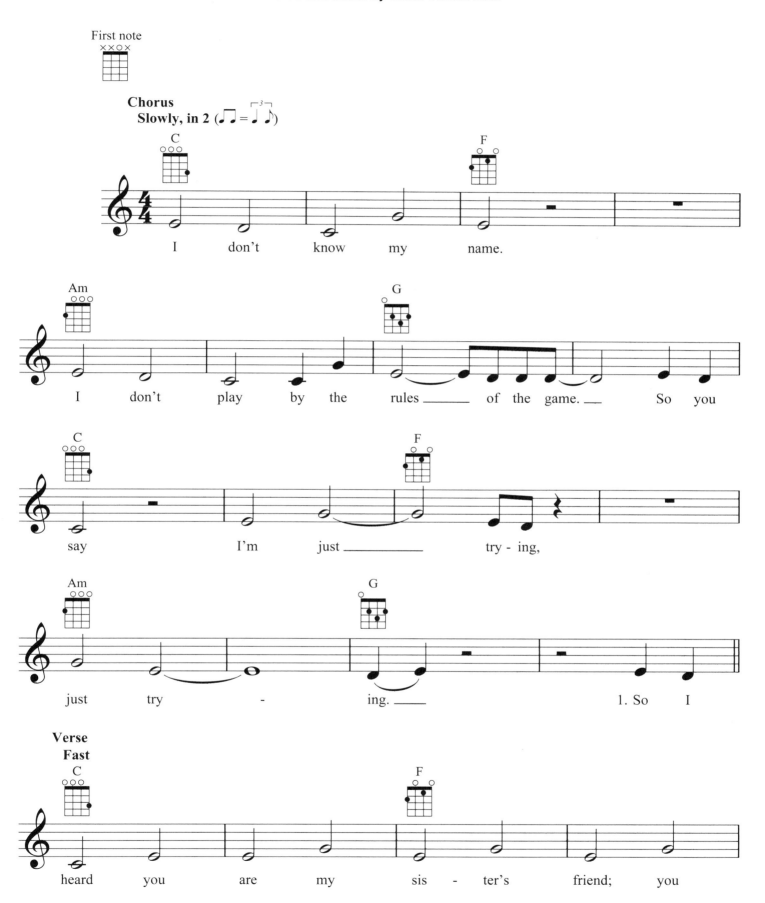

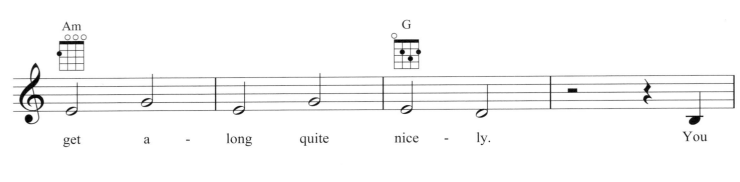

get a - long quite nice - ly. You

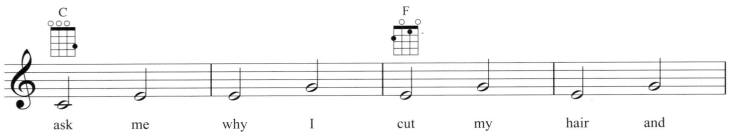

ask me why I cut my hair and

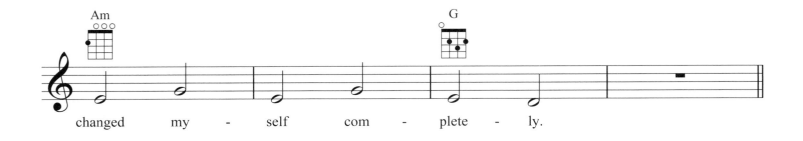

changed my - self com - plete - ly.

𝄋 **Chorus**
Moderately fast

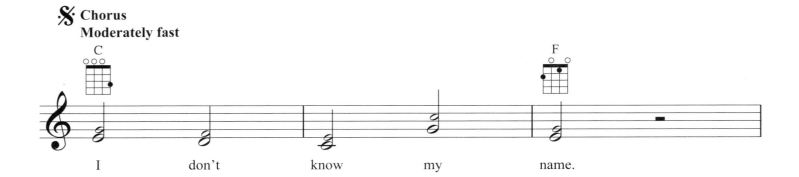

I don't know my name.

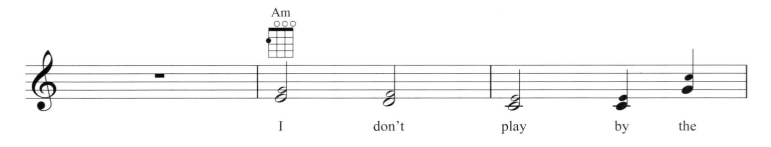

I don't play by the

rules _____ of the game. _____ So you say

I'm just _____ try - ing,

just try - ing. ____ 2. I

Verse
Very fast

went from bland and pop - u - lar to

Moderately fast

join - ing the march - ing ____ band. I

made the clos - est friends I'll ev - er

have in my _____ life - time. ____

To Coda

rit.

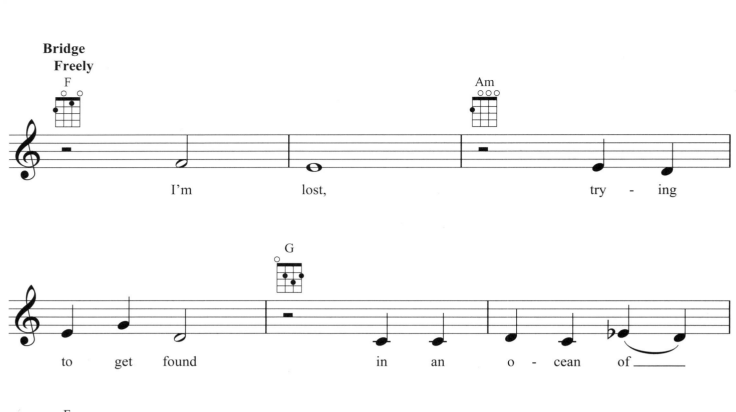

I'm lost, try - ing

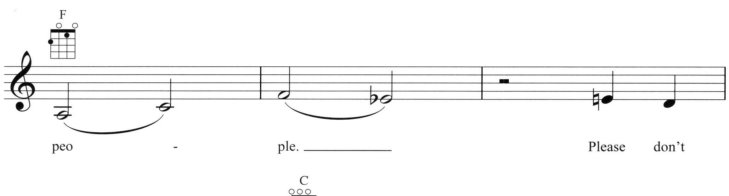

to get found in an o - cean of _____

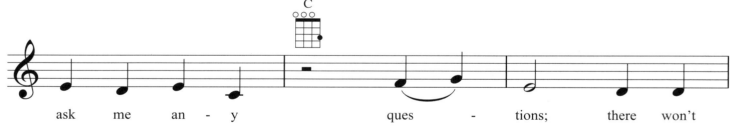

peo - ple. _____ Please don't

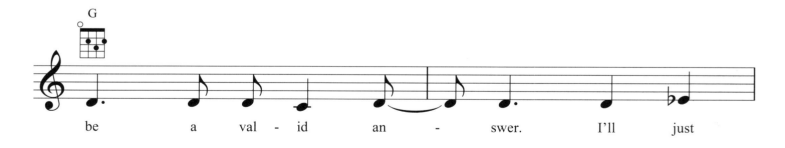

ask me an - y ques - tions; there won't

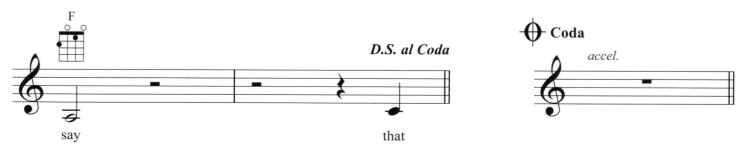

be a val - id an - swer. I'll just

say that

D.S. al Coda

Coda

accel.

Home

Words and Music by Greg Holden and Drew Pearson

just know you're

not a - lone, _____ 'cause I'm gon - na

make this place your _____ home.

%. Verse

Set - tle down, _____

it - 'll all be _____ clear.

Don't pay _____ no mind to _____ the de - mons; they

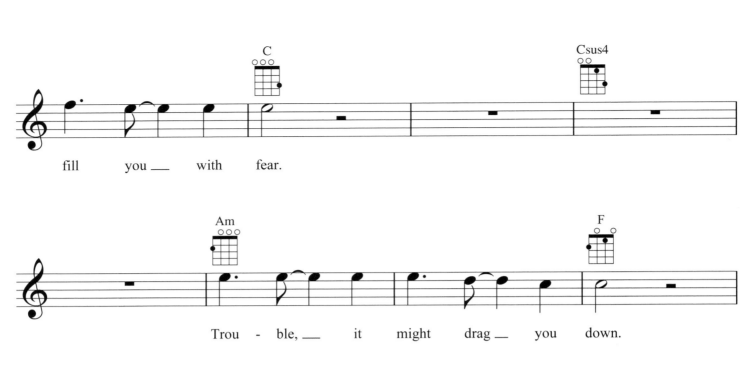

fill   you —   with   fear.

Trou - ble, —   it   might   drag —   you   down.

You —   get   lost,   you —   can   al - ways —   be   found.

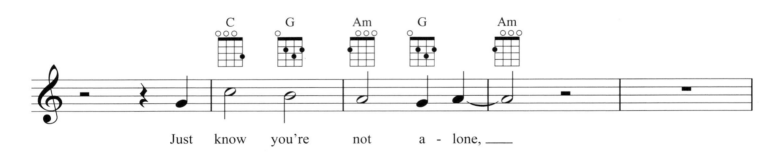

Just   know   you're   not   a - lone, ____

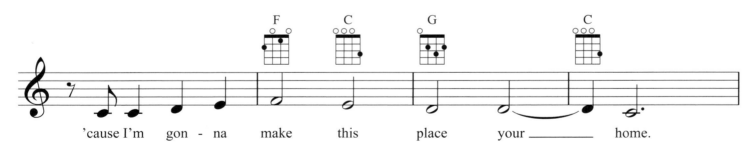

'cause I'm   gon - na   make   this   place   your _____ home.

Interlude

1. Ooh, _____
2.–5. Ah, _____

110

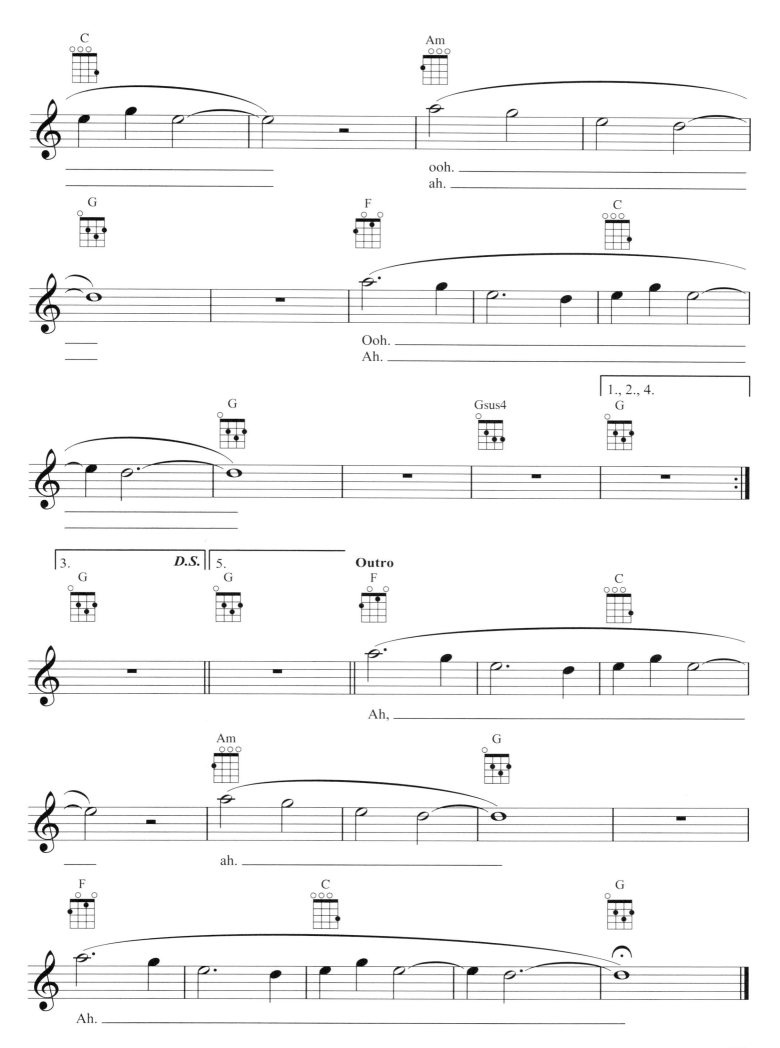

ooh.

ah.

Ooh.

Ah.

1., 2., 4.

3. *D.S.* 5. **Outro**

Ah,

ah.

Ah.

111

I Knew You Were Trouble

Words and Music by Taylor Swift, Shellback and Max Martin

I Took a Pill in Ibiza

Words and Music by Mike Posner

Pre-Chorus

To Coda ⊕

Chorus

117

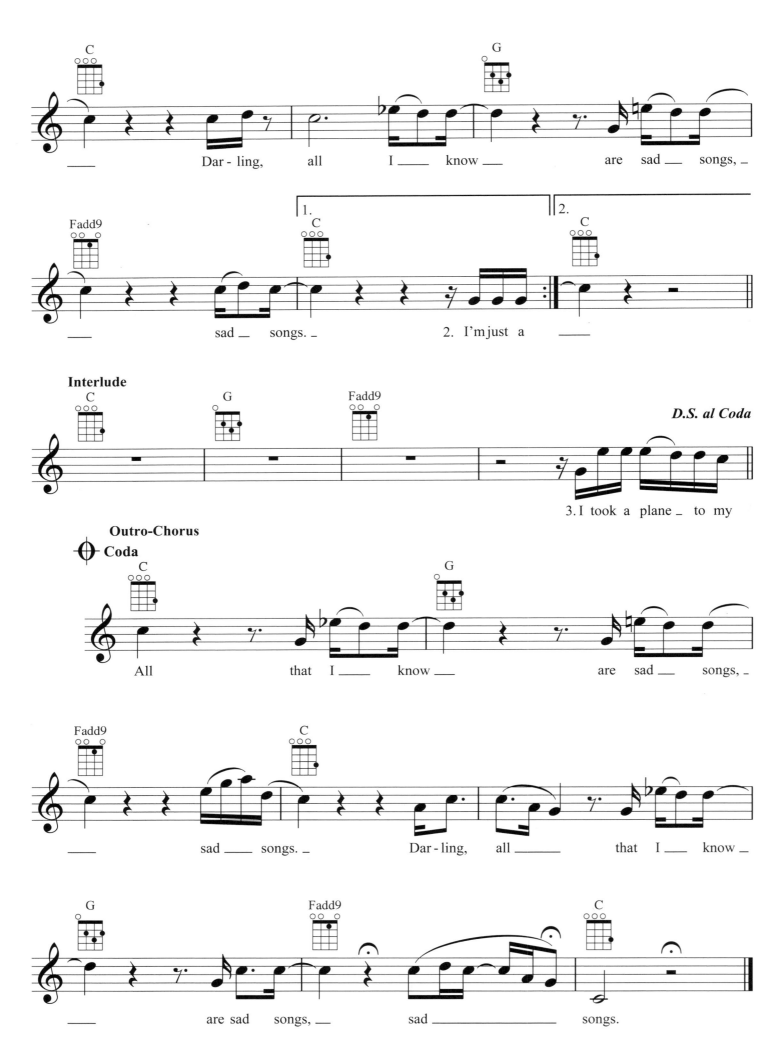

Dar - ling, all I know are sad songs,

1. sad songs.

2. I'm just a

Interlude

D.S. al Coda

3. I took a plane to my

Outro-Chorus
Coda

All that I know are sad songs,

sad songs. Dar - ling, all that I know

are sad songs, sad songs.

Just Give Me a Reason

Words and Music by Alecia Moore, Jeff Bhasker and Nate Ruess

120

thought that we were fine. _____ *Female:* Oh, we had ev - 'ry - thing. Your

head is run - ning wild ___ a - gain. My dear, we still have ev -'ry - thing, and

it's all in ___ your mind. *Female:* Yeah, but this is hap - pen - ing.

Pre-Chorus

Male:
You've been hav - ing real bad dreams, oh, oh. You used to lie so close to

me, oh, oh. *Both:* There's noth - ing more than emp - ty sheets be - tween our

love, our ___ love, oh, ___ our love, our

Chorus

love. _____ *Both:* Just give me a rea - son, just a lit - tle bit's e - nough, just a

sec - ond. We're not bro - ken, just bent, _____ and we can learn to love a - gain. __

Male:
____ I nev - er stopped; you're still writ - ten in the scars on my heart.

Both: You're not bro - ken, just bent, _____ and we can learn to love a - gain. __

Bridge

Female:
_____ Oh, tear ducts and rust. __ *Male:* I'll fix it for us. _____ *Female:* We're col - lect - ing dust, __

____ but our love's ___ e - nough. _____ *Male:* You're hold - ing it in. __

123

I Will Wait

Words and Music by Mumford & Sons

I Won't Give Up

Words and Music by Jason Mraz and Michael Natter

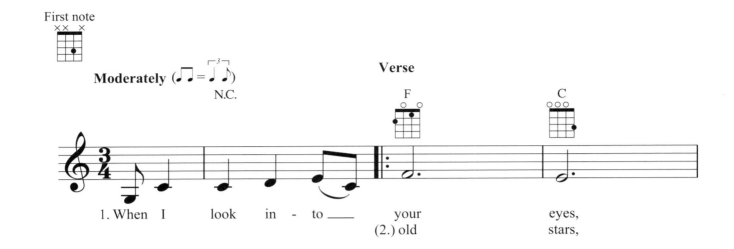

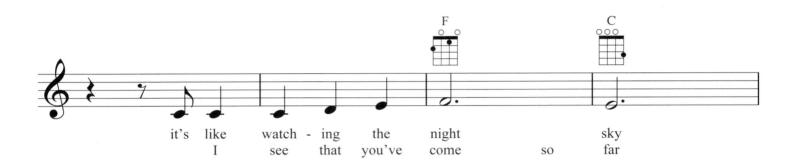

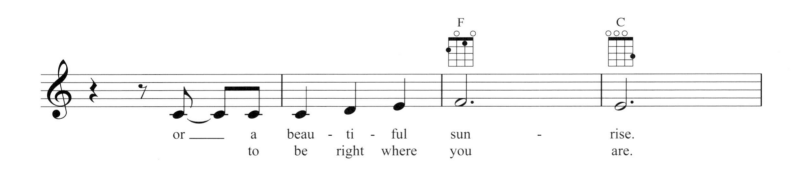

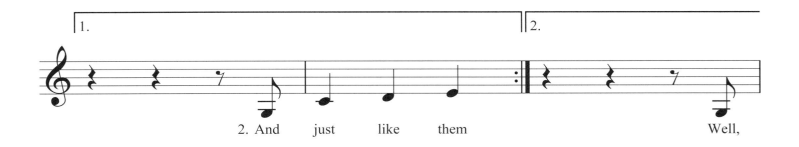

2. And just like them Well,

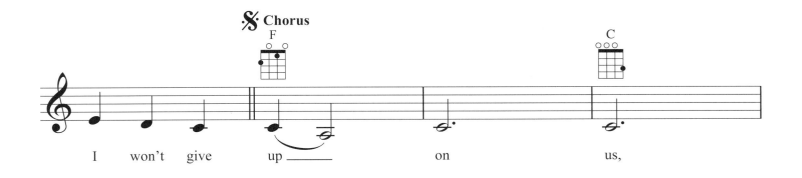

%. **Chorus**

F   C

I won't give up _____ on us,

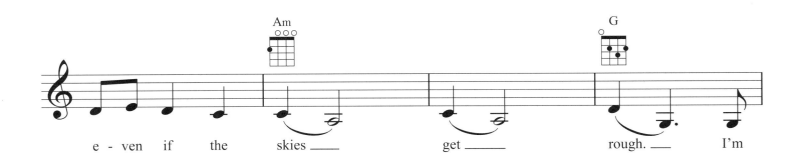

Am   G

e - ven if the skies ___ get ___ rough. ___ I'm

F   C

giv - ing ___ you all _____ my love. _____ I'm

To Coda ⊕ G

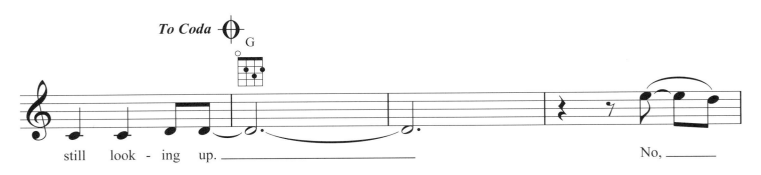

still look - ing up. _____ No, ___

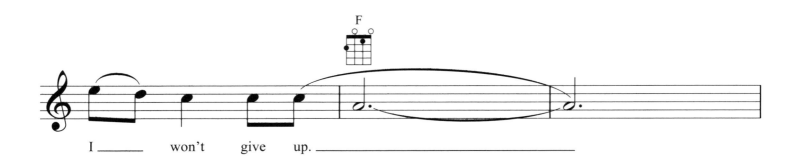

I _____ won't give up. _____

Bridge

I don't wan - na be some - one who
dif - f'renc - es, they do a

walks a - way so eas - i - ly. I'm here to stay and make the dif - fer - ence that
lot to teach us how to use the tools and gifts we got; yeah, we got a

I can make. _____ Our
lot at stake. _____

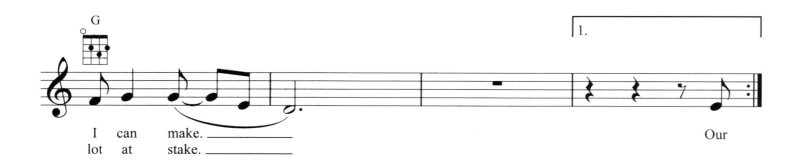

And in the end, you're still my friend; at least we did in - tend for

us   to   work. We   did - n't   break, we   did - n't   burn.   We   had   to   learn

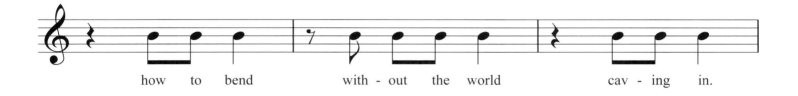

how   to   bend   with - out   the   world   cav - ing   in.

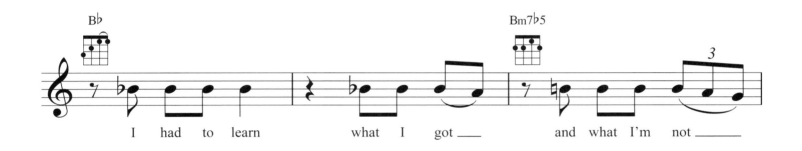

I   had   to   learn   what   I   got ___   and   what   I'm   not ___

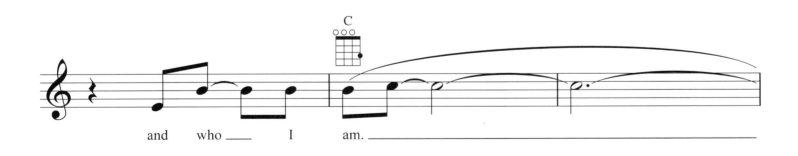

and   who ___   I   am. ___

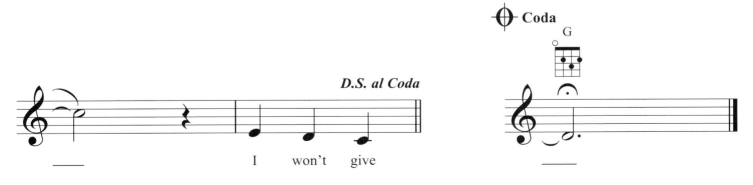

___   I   won't   give   ___

The Lazy Song

Words and Music by Bruno Mars, Ari Levine, Philip Lawrence and Keinan Warsame

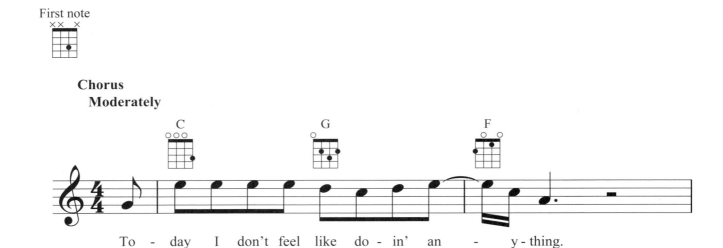

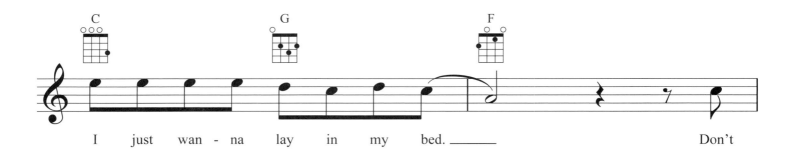

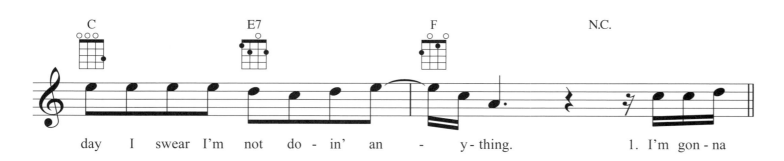

Pre-Chorus

yes, I said it, I said it, I said it 'cause __ I can. __ To-

Chorus

day I don't feel like do - in' an - y - thing.

I just wan - na lay in my bed. _____ Don't

feel like pick- in' up ____ my phone, so leave a mes - sage at the tone 'cause to-

1., 3.

day I swear I'm not do - in' an - y - thing, noth - ing at all. __

To Coda

____ (Woo, hoo, __ woo, hoo, __ hoo.) ____ Noth-ing at all. ____ (Woo, hoo, __ woo, hoo, __

hoo.) _____   2. To - mor - row   - y - thing,   No,   I

Bridge

ain't   gon - na comb   my   hair,   'cause   I   ain't go - in'   an - y - where,

no,   no,   no,   no,   no,   no,   no, ___   no,   no,   oh.   I'll   just

strut   in   my birth - day   suit   and   let   ev - 'ry - thing _   hang   loose. _____

D.S. al Coda
(take 1st ending)

Yeah, yeah, yeah, yeah, yeah, yeah, yeah, _ yeah, yeah,   yeah.   Oh, _____   to -

Coda

hoo.) _____   Noth - ing   at   all. _____

Let Her Go

Words and Music by Michael David Rosenberg

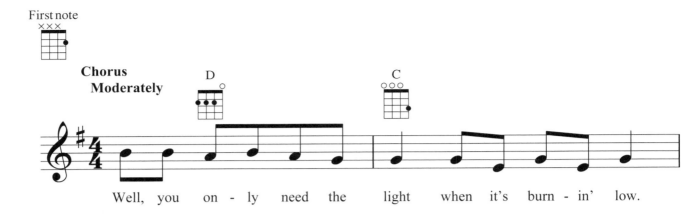

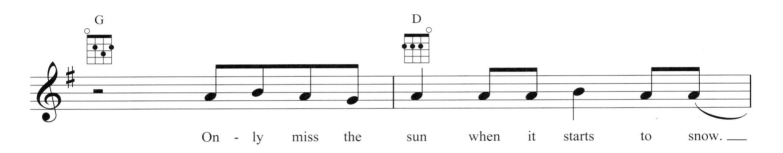

love her when you let her go.

And you let her go. ___

Verse

1. Star-ing at the bot-tom of your glass hop-ing one ___ day you'll make a dream
2. Star-ing at the ceil-ing in the dark, same old emp - ty feel-ing in your

last. But dreams come slow ___ and they go so ___ fast.
heart. 'Cause love comes slow ___ and it goes so ___ fast.

You see her when you close ___ your
Well, you see her when you fall ___ a -

eyes. May-be one ___ day you'll un-der-stand why ev-'ry-thing you
sleep and nev-er to touch ___ and nev-er to keep. 'Cause you loved her too ___

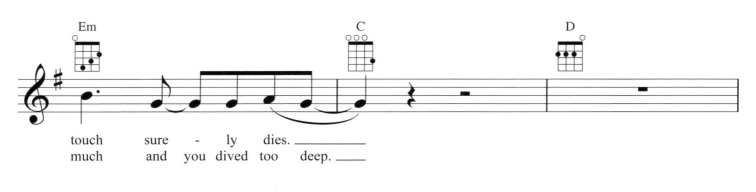

touch   sure - ly dies. _____
much   and you dived too deep. _____

𝄋 **Chorus**

But
Well, } you on - ly need the   light when it's burn-in' low.   On - ly miss the

sun when it starts to snow. __   On - ly know you   love her when you let her go.

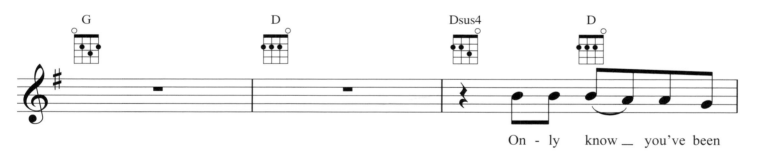

On - ly   know __ you've been

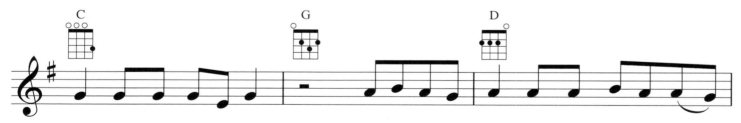

high when you're feel - in' low.   On - ly hate the   road when you're miss - in' home. __

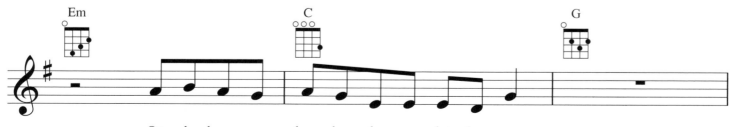

On - ly know you   love her when you let her go.

138

Love Yourself

Words and Music by Justin Bieber, Benjamin Levin,
Ed Sheeran, Joshua Gudwin and Scott Braun

Pre-Chorus 1

write a song — 'cause I did-n't want an-y-one think-ing I still care. I

don't, but you still hit my phone up. And, ba - by, I'll be

mov-ing on, — and I think it should be some-thing I don't wan-na

hold back. May - be you should know that my ma - ma don't

Pre-Chorus 2

like — you, and she likes ev-er-y-one. — And I — nev-er

like — to ad - mit that I — was wrong. — And I've been so

to let you break down my walls? ____ 'Cause if you

Outro-Chorus

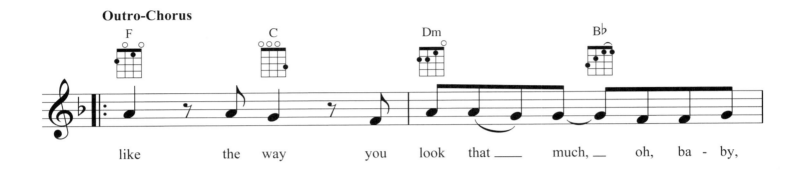

like the way you look that ___ much, __ oh, ba - by,

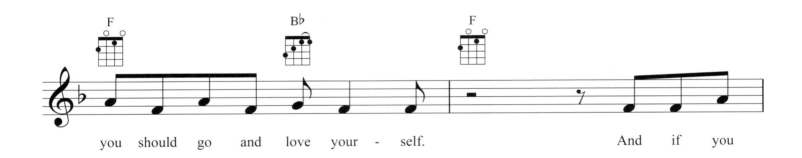

you should go and love your - self. And if you

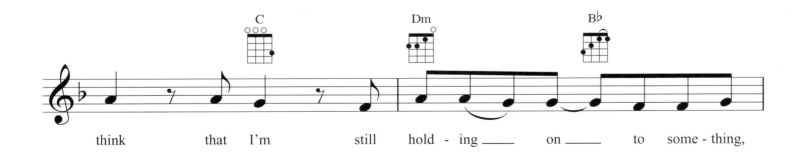

think that I'm still hold - ing ____ on ____ to some - thing,

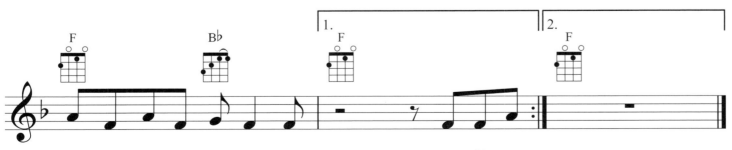

you should go and love your - self. 'Cause if you

Let It Go

Words and Music by James Bay and Paul Barry

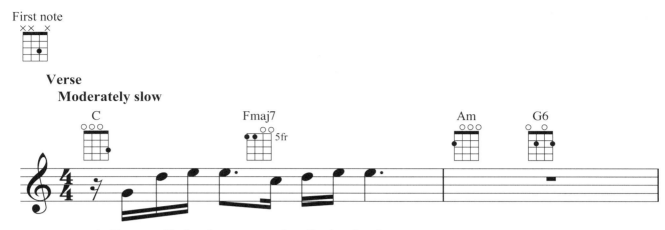

1. From walk-ing home   and   talk-ing loads,

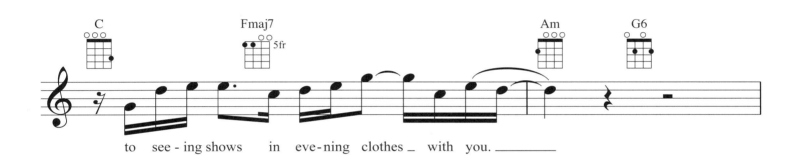

to   see - ing shows   in   eve-ning clothes _ with   you. _____

From   nerv - ous   touch   and   get - ting drunk,

to   stay - ing up   and   wak - ing up _____ with   you. _____   But   now we're

§ **Pre-Chorus**

sleep-ing at the edge, hold-ing some-thing we don't _ need. ___
rec - og-nize my-self; it's fun - ny how re - flec-tions _ change. _
All this de-
When we're be-

lu - sion in our heads is gon - na bring us to our _ knees. _
com-ing some-thing else, I think it's time to walk a - way. ___
So, come on, let it

Chorus

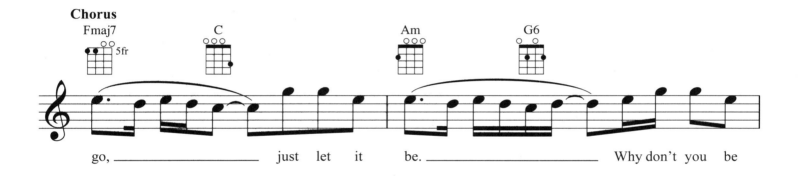

go, _____ just let it be. _____ Why don't you be

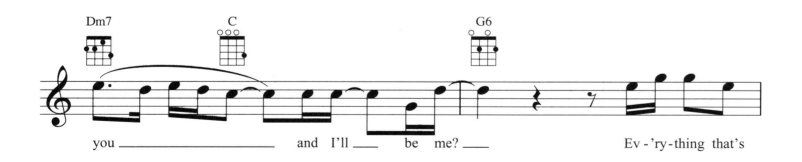

you _____ and I'll ___ be me? ___
Ev -'ry-thing that's

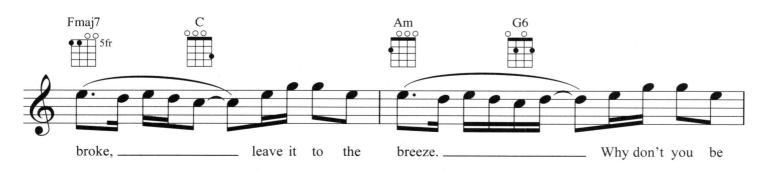

broke, _____ leave it to the breeze. _____ Why don't you be

146

you _____ and I'll ____ be me? ____   And I'll _____ be me. _

Am G6   C   Fmaj7   Am G6

To Coda ⊕ **Verse**

2. From throw-ing clothes a - cross the floor,

to teeth and claws,   and slam-ming doors ___ at you. _____

If this is all we're liv - ing for, ____   why are we

D.S. al Coda

do - ing it, do - ing it, do - ing it an - y-more?   I used to

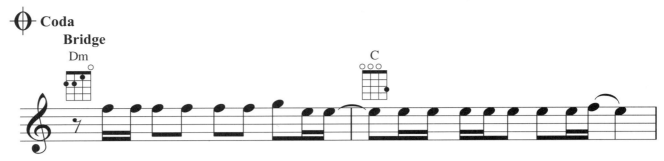

⊕ Coda
Bridge

Tryin' to fit your hand in-side of mine ___ when we know it just don't be-long. _

There's no force on earth ___ could make it feel right, ___ no. ___ Whoa. ___

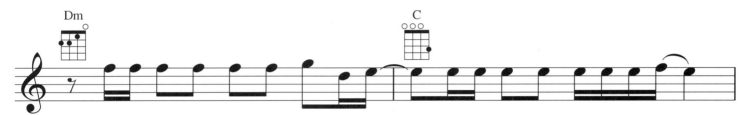

Tryin' to push this prob-lem up the hill ___ when it's just too heav-y to hold. _

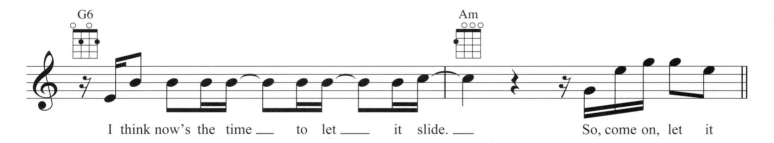

I think now's the time ___ to let ___ it slide. ___ So, come on, let it

Chorus

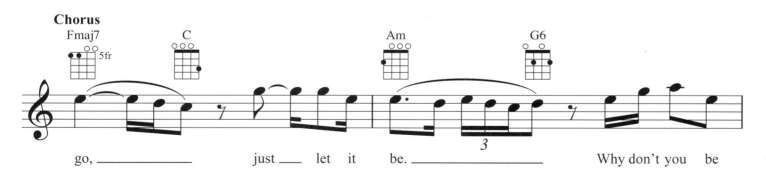

go, ___ just ___ let it be. ___ Why don't you be

you ___ and I'll ___ be me? ___ Ev-'ry-thing that's

The Middle

Words and Music by Sarah Aarons, Marcus Lomax, Jordan Johnson, Anton Zaslavski, Kyle Trewartha, Michael Trewartha and Stefan Johnson

1. Take a seat right o - ver there, sat on the stairs.

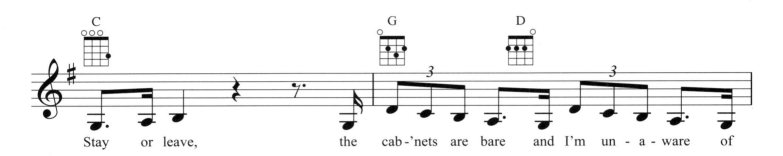

Stay or leave, the cab -'nets are bare and I'm un - a - ware of

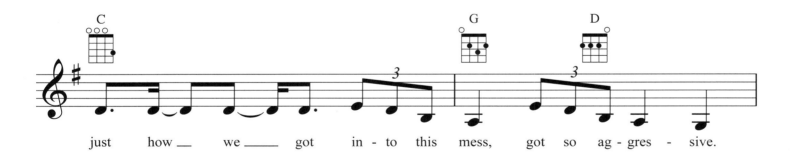

just how __ we __ got in - to this mess, got so ag - gres - sive.

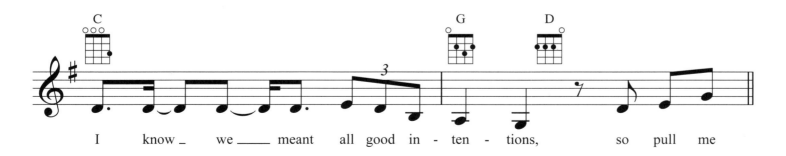

I know __ we __ meant all good in - ten - tions, so pull me

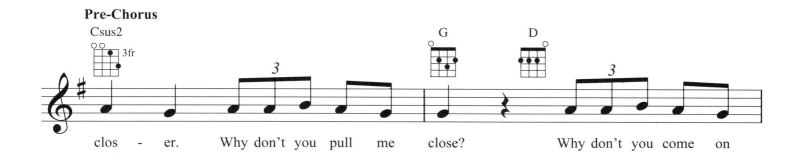

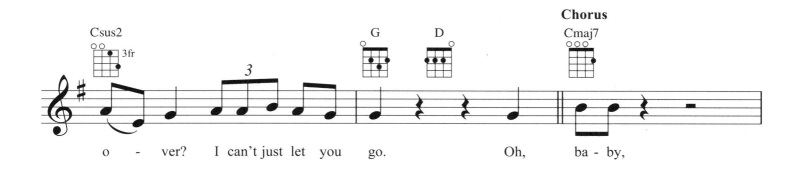

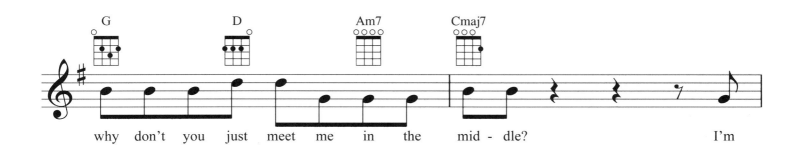

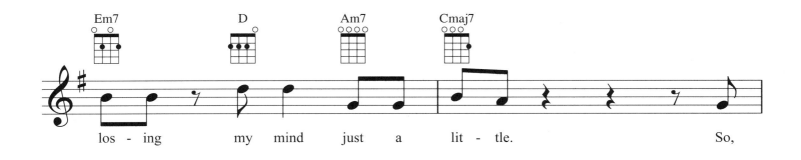

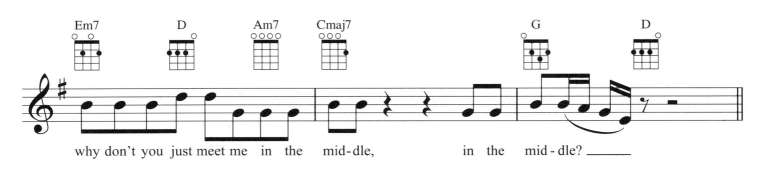

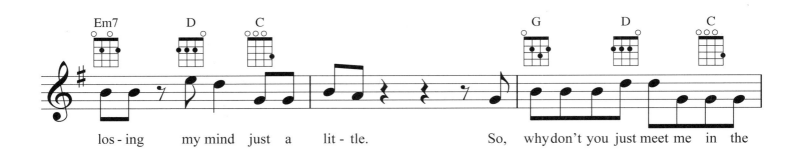

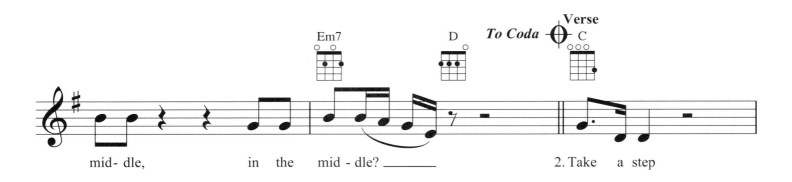

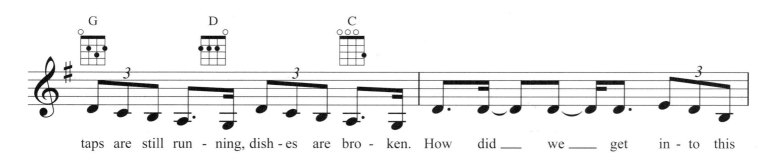

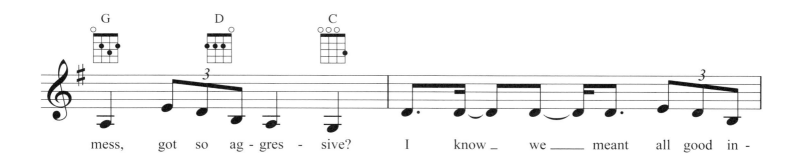

mess, got so ag - gres - sive? I know __ we ____ meant all good in -

Pre-Chorus

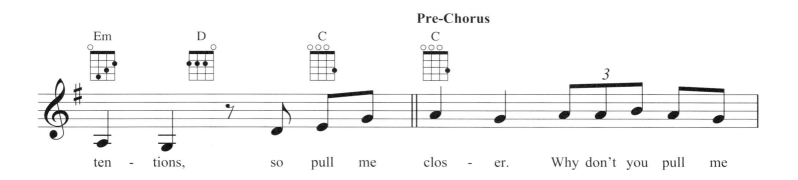

ten - tions, so pull me clos - er. Why don't you pull me

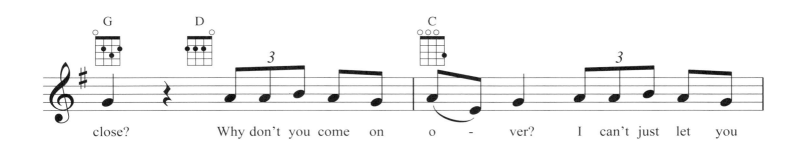

close? Why don't you come on o - ver? I can't just let you

D.S. al Coda

Bridge
Coda

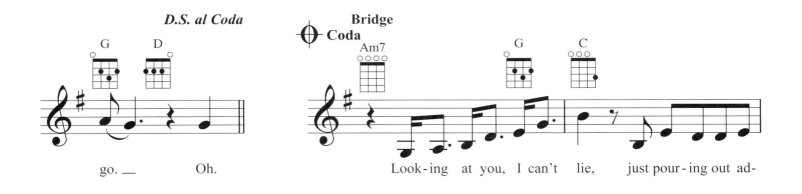

go. __ Oh. Look - ing at you, I can't lie, just pour - ing out ad -

mis - sion, __ re - gard - less of my ob - jec - tion. __ Oh, oh,

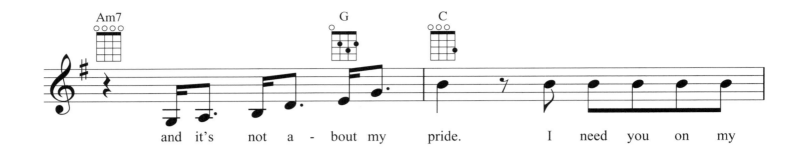

and it's not a - bout my pride. I need you on my

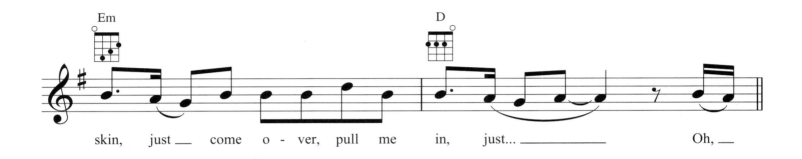

skin, just ___ come o - ver, pull me in, just... _____ Oh, ___

Chorus

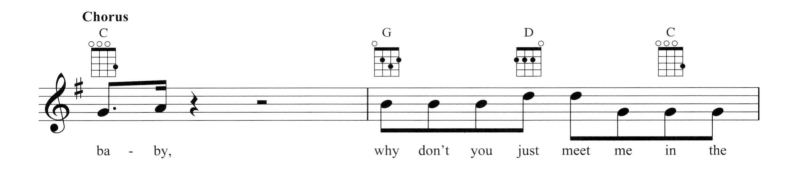

ba - by, why don't you just meet me in the

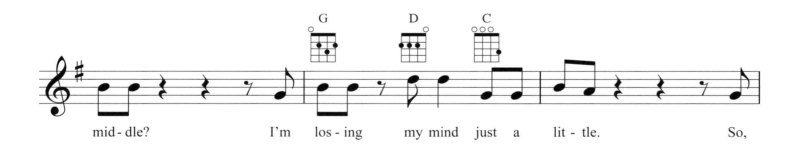

mid - dle? I'm los - ing my mind just a lit - tle. So,

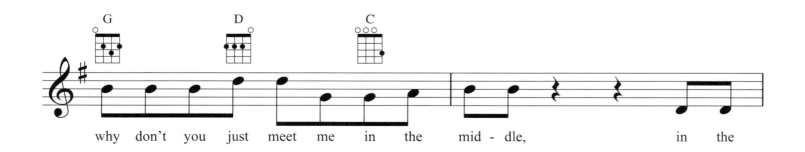

why don't you just meet me in the mid - dle, in the

Outro-Chorus

(with vocal ad lib.)

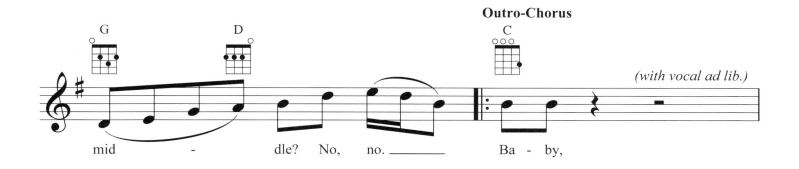

mid - dle? No, no. _____ Ba - by,

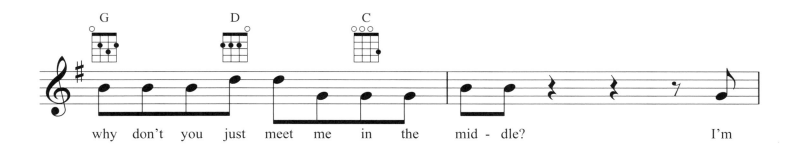

why don't you just meet me in the mid - dle? I'm

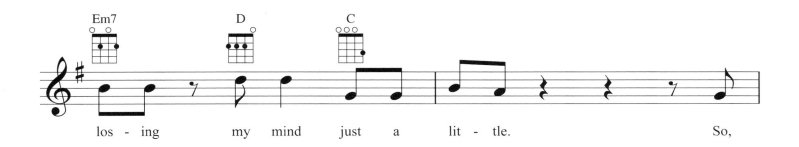

los - ing my mind just a lit - tle. So,

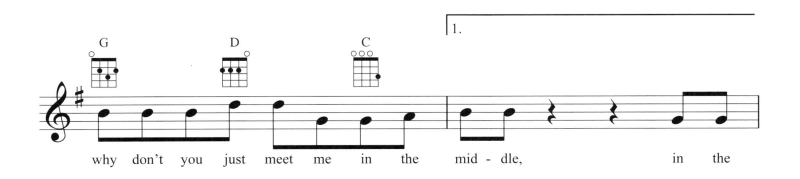

why don't you just meet me in the mid - dle, in the

mid - dle? mid - dle, mid - dle, in the mid - dle, mid - dle?

155

Old Town Road
(Remix)

Words and Music by Trent Reznor, Billy Ray Cyrus, Jocelyn Donald,
Atticus Ross, Kiowa Roukema and Montero Lamar Hill

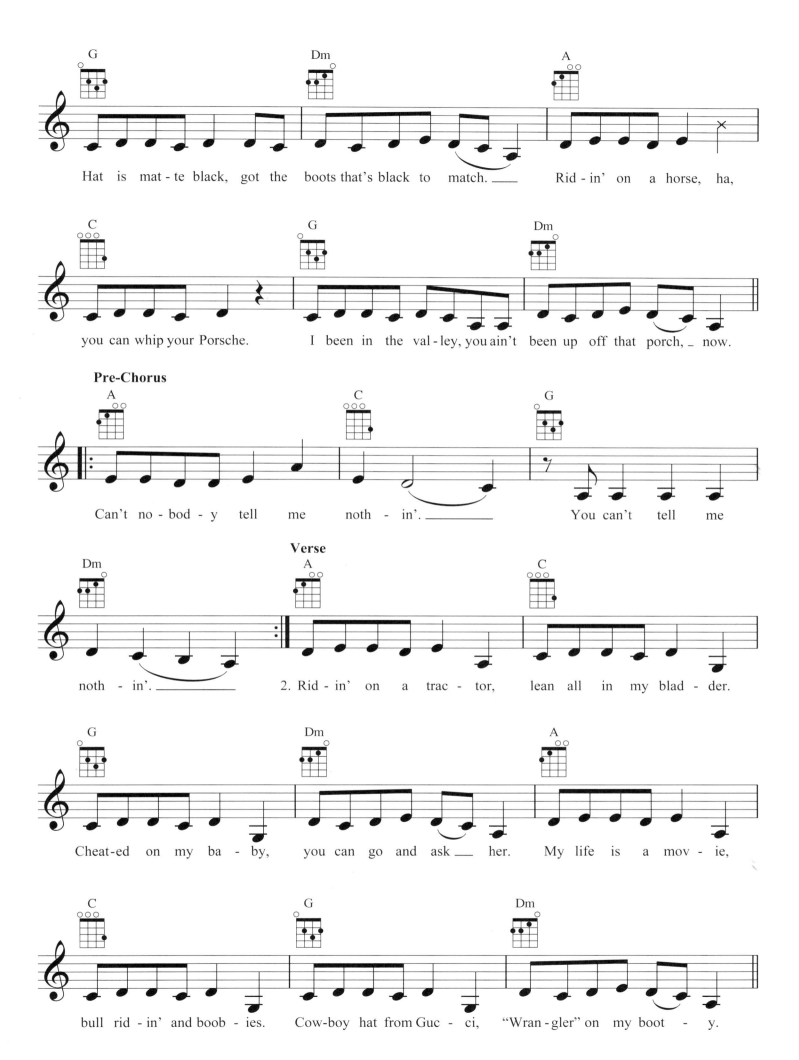

Ma - se - ra - ti sports car. Got no stress; I've been through _ all that. _ I'm like a

Marl - boro Man, so I kick ___ on back. _ Wish I could roll on back to that old _

___ town road. _ I wan - na ride till I can't no more.
Yeah, ___ I'm gon - na

Chorus

take my horse to the old town road. _ I'm gon-na ride till I can't no more. I'm gon-na

take my horse to the old town road. _ I'm gon-na ride till I can't no more.

Outro

Repeat and fade

(Instrumental)

159

Paradise

Words and Music by Guy Berryman, Jon Buckland, Will Champion, Chris Martin and Brian Eno

par - a - par - a - - par - a - dise ev - 'ry time she closed __ her __ eyes.

Interlude

Ooh, _____ ooh. _____

Verse

2. When she was just a girl, _____ she ex - pect - ed the world. __

_____ But it flew a - way from her reach, _____ and the

bul - lets catch in her teeth. _____ Life goes on, it gets __

__ so heav - y, the wheel __ breaks the but - ter - fly.

par - a - par - a - par - a - dise, par - a - par - a - - par - a - dise, par - a - par - a - par - a - dise.

Bridge

Oh, _____ oh. _____ La, la, _____ la, la, la,

la, la, _____ la, la, la, la, la, _____ la, la, la, _____ la, la. _____ And so ly -

- ing un - der - neath _____ those storm - y skies, _____

she said, "Oh, _____ I know the

Radioactive

Words and Music by Daniel Reynolds, Benjamin McKee, Daniel Sermon, Alexander Grant and Josh Mosser

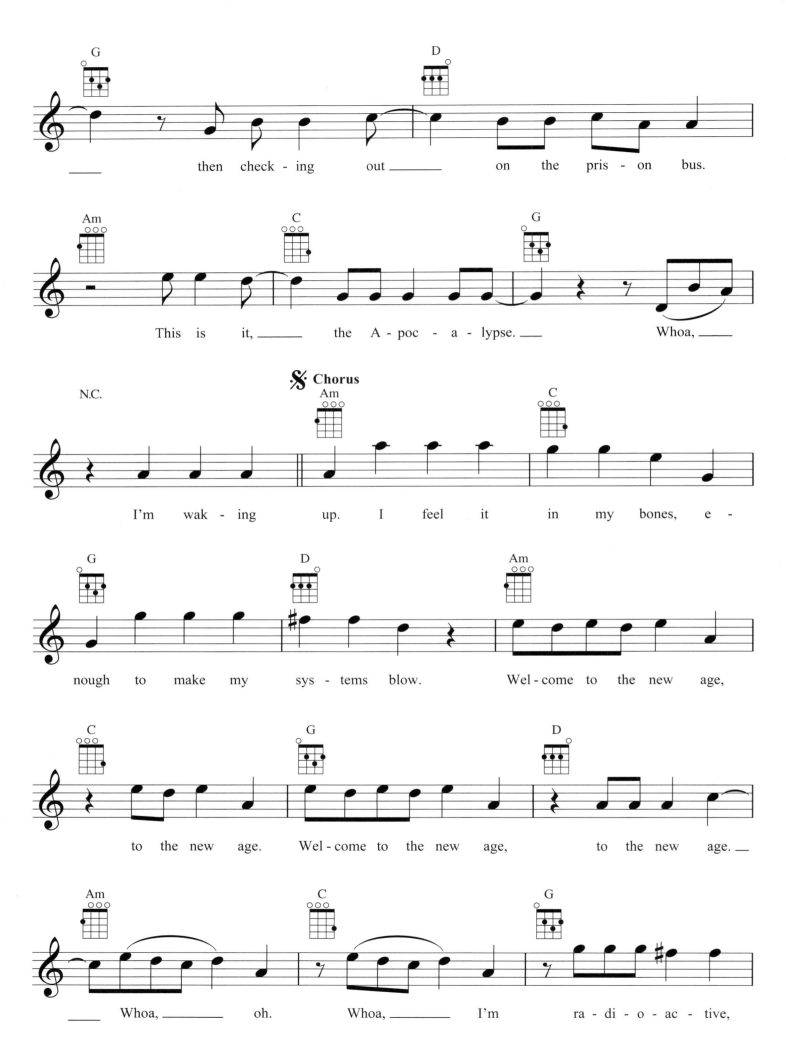

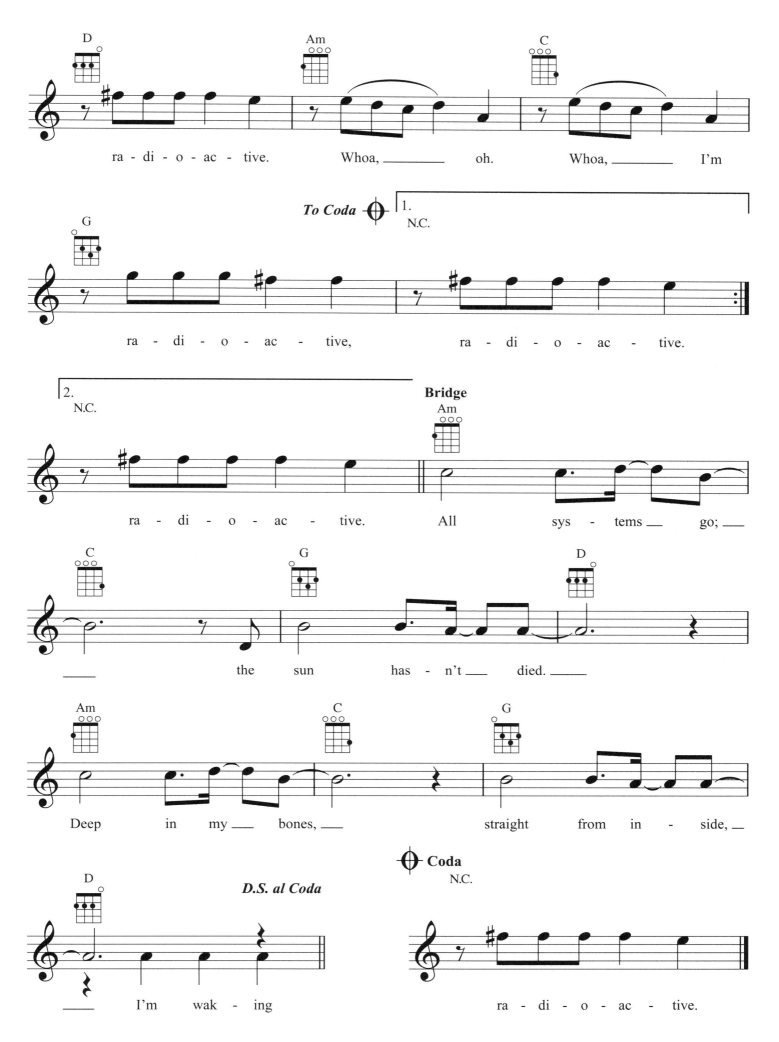

Riptide

Words and Music by Vance Joy

come un - stuck. ___ La - dy, ___ run-ning down ___ to the

rip - tide, tak-en a-way ___ to the dark side, I wan-na be ___ your

left - hand ___ man. ___ I love you when you're sing - ing that

song, ___ and I got a lump ___ in my throat 'cause you're gon-na sing ___ the words ___

1.
___ wrong.

2.
___ wrong.

(Instrumental)

Bridge

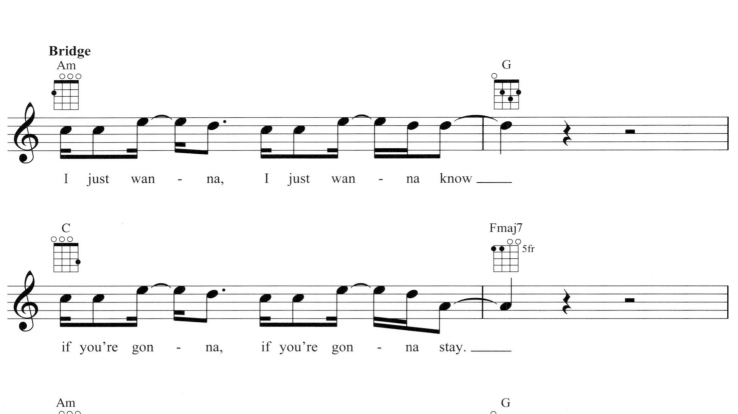

I just wan - na, I just wan - na know ___

if you're gon - na, if you're gon - na stay. ___

I just got - ta, I just got - ta know; ___

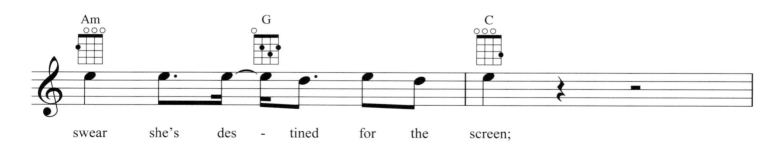

I can't have ___ it, I can't have ___ it an - y oth - er way. I

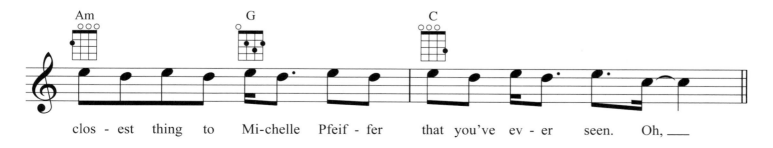

swear she's des - tined for the screen;

clos - est thing to Mi-chelle Pfeif - fer that you've ev - er seen. Oh, ___

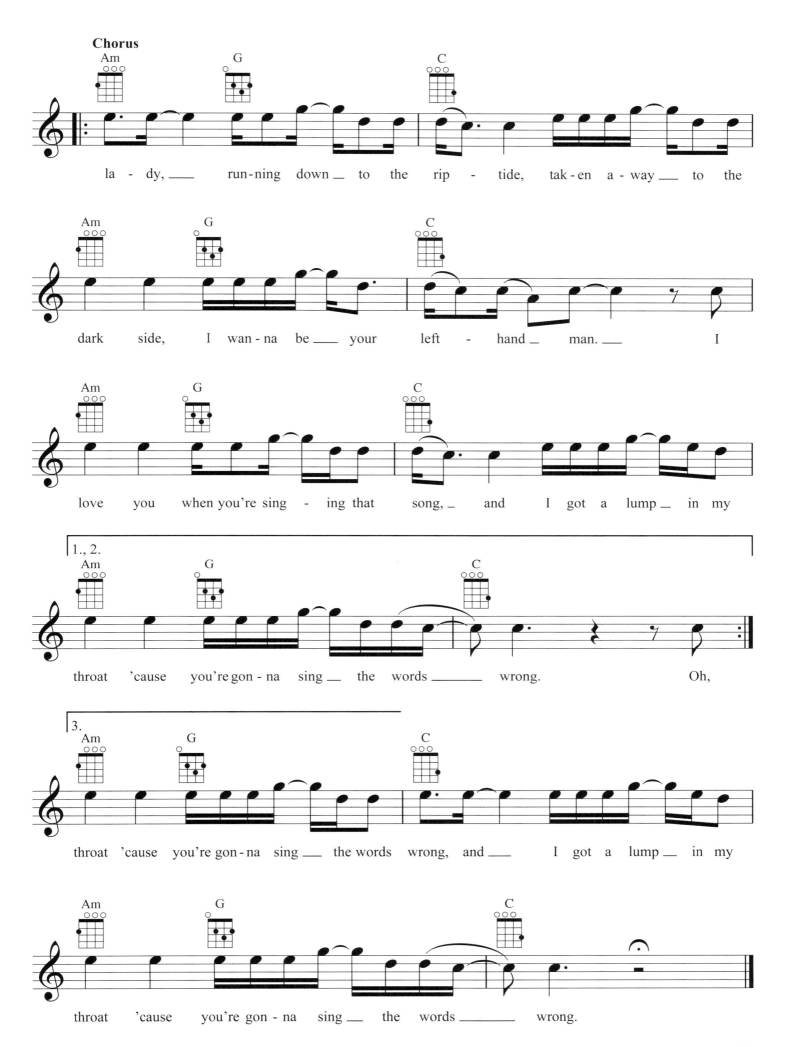

Rude

Words and Music by Nasri Atweh, Mark Pellizzer, Alex Tanas, Ben Spivak and Adam Messinger

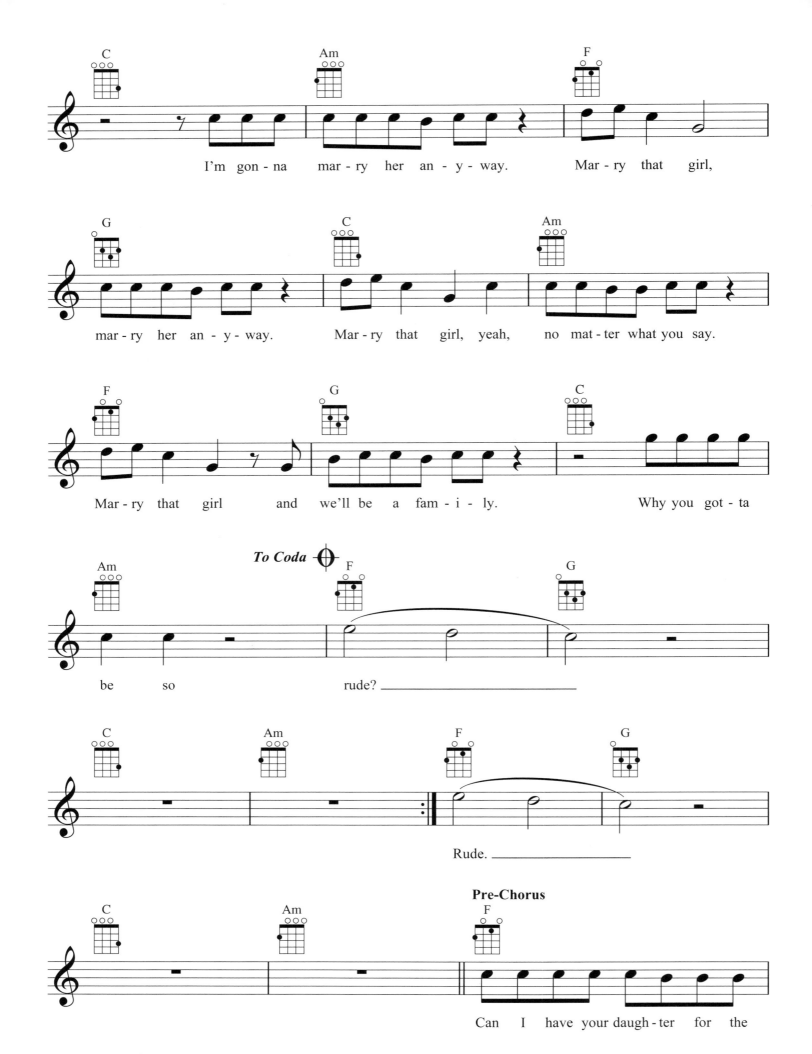

Say You Won't Let Go

Words and Music by Steven Solomon, James Arthur and Neil Ormandy

First note

Verse
Moderately fast

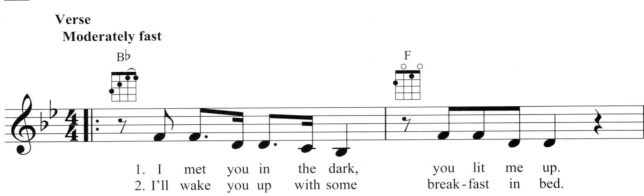

1. I met you in the dark, you lit me up.
2. I'll wake you up with some break-fast in bed.

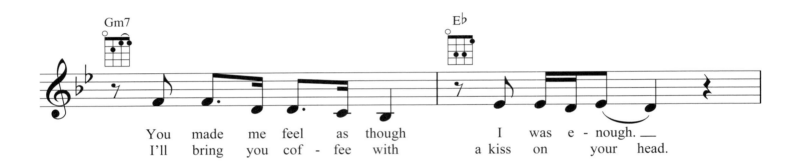

You made me feel as though I was e-nough.
I'll bring you cof-fee with a kiss on your head.

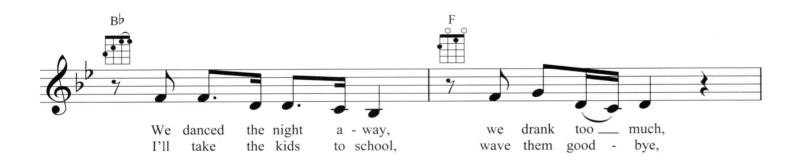

We danced the night a-way, we drank too much,
I'll take the kids to school, wave them good-bye,

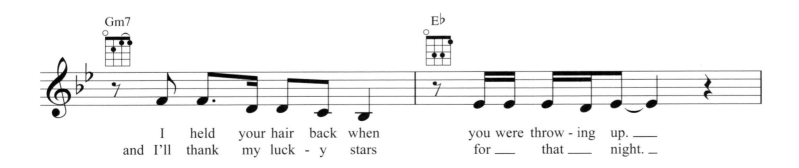

I held your hair back when you were throw-ing up.
and I'll thank my luck-y stars for that night.

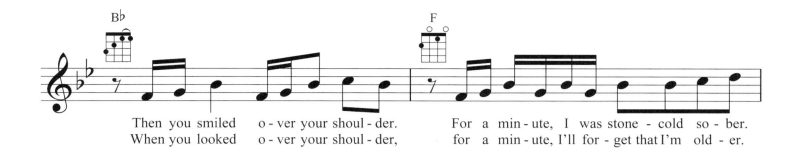

Then you smiled o - ver your shoul - der.   For a min - ute, I was stone - cold so - ber.
When you looked o - ver your shoul - der,   for a min - ute, I'll for - get that I'm old - er.

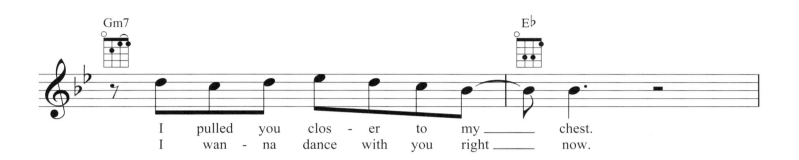

I pulled you clos - er to my _____ chest.
I wan - na dance with you right _____ now.

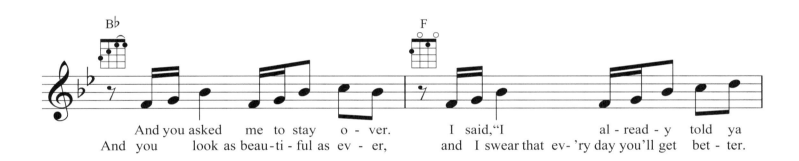

And you asked me to stay o - ver.   I said, "I al - read - y told ya
And you look as beau - ti - ful as ev - er,   and I swear that ev - 'ry day you'll get bet - ter.

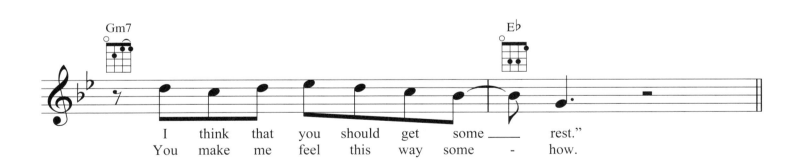

I think that you should get some _____ rest."
You make me feel this way some - how.

Pre-Chorus

I knew I loved you then,   but you'd nev - er know,
I'm so in love with you,   and I hope you know,
I'm gon - na love you till   my lungs give out.

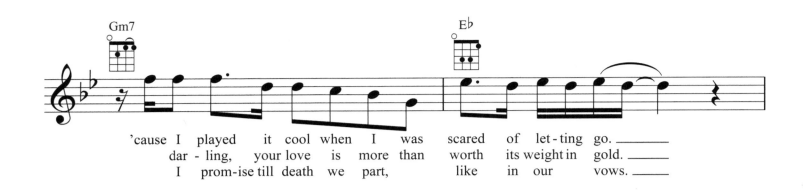

'cause I played it cool when I was scared of let-ting go. ____
dar - ling, your love is more than worth its weight in gold. ____
I prom-ise till death we part, like in our vows. ____

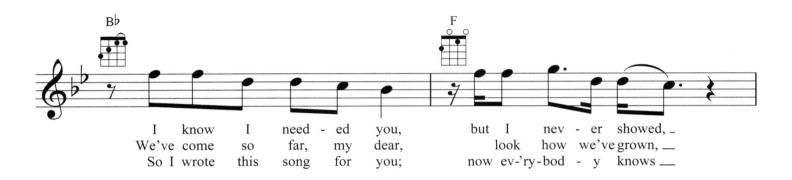

I know I need - ed you, but I nev - er showed, __
We've come so far, my dear, look how we've grown, __
So I wrote this song for you; now ev-'ry-bod - y knows __

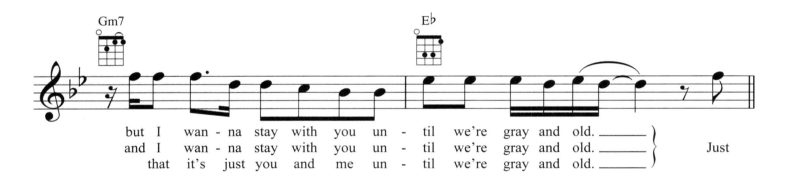

but I wan - na stay with you un - til we're gray and old. ____)
and I wan - na stay with you un - til we're gray and old. ____ } Just
that it's just you and me un - til we're gray and old. ____)

Chorus

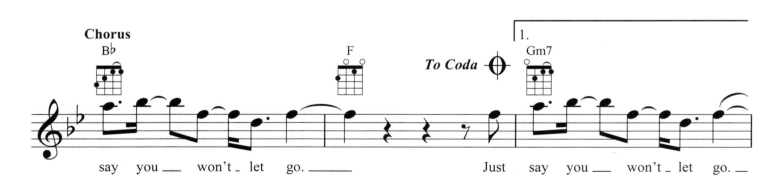

say you __ won't _ let go. ____   Just say you __ won't _ let go. __

____   say you __ won't _ let go. ____

178

Bridge

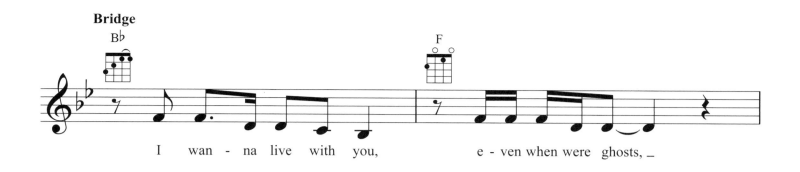

I wan - na live with you, e - ven when were ghosts, __

D.S. al Coda

'cause you were al - ways there for me when I need-ed you most. _____

Coda

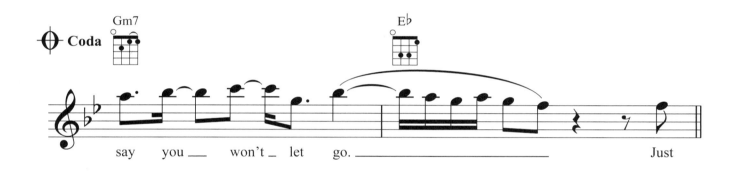

say you __ won't __ let go. _____ Just

Outro-Chorus

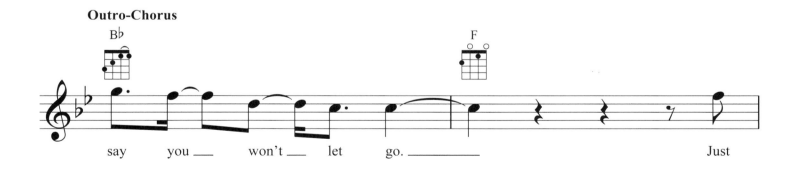

say you __ won't __ let go. _____ Just

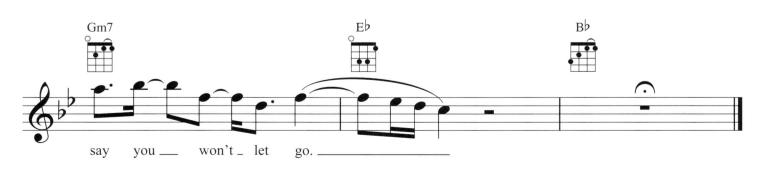

say you __ won't __ let go. _____

Señorita

Words and Music by Camila Cabello, Charlotte Aitchison, Jack Patterson, Shawn Mendes,
Magnus Høiberg, Benjamin Levin, Ali Tamposi and Andrew Wotman

rain. Sweat drip - pin' off me. ___ Be - fore I e - ven knew her

name, la, ___ la, la, it felt like ooh, la, ___ la, la. Yeah, ___

___ no. ___ Sap - phire ___ moon - light,

we danced for hours ___ in the sand. Te - qui - la sun - rise,

her bod - y fit right in my hands, la, ___ la, la. It felt like

ooh, la, ___ la, la, yeah. ___ *Both:* I love it when you

call me "se - ño - ri - ta." I wish I could pre - tend I did - n't need _

_ ya, but ev - 'ry touch is ooh, la, _ la, la. It's true, la, _ la, la. Ooh, _

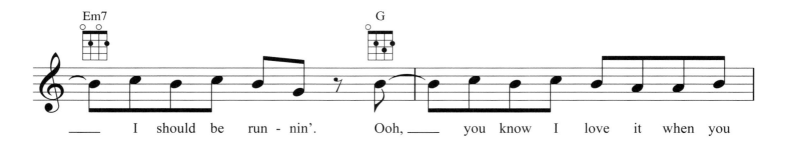

_ I should be run - nin'. Ooh, _ you know I love it when you

call me "se - ño - ri - ta." I wish it was - n't so damn hard to leave _

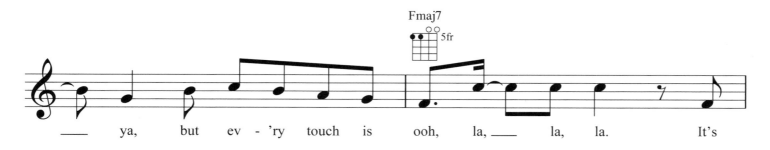

_ ya, but ev - 'ry touch is ooh, la, _ la, la. It's

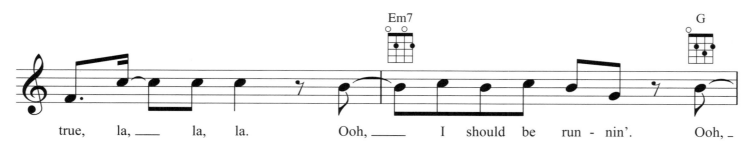

true, la, _ la, la. Ooh, _ I should be run - nin'. Ooh, _

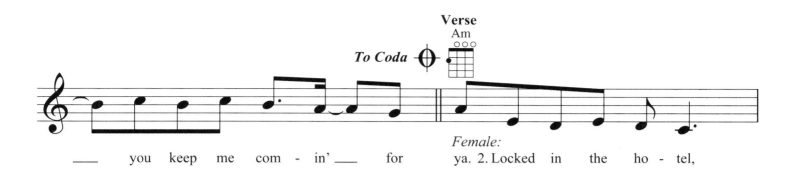

_you keep me com-in' _ for ya. 2. Locked in the ho-tel,

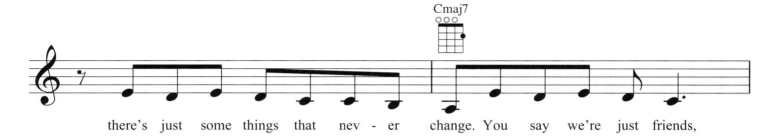

there's just some things that nev-er change. You say we're just friends,

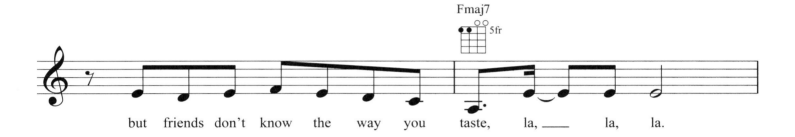

but friends don't know the way you taste, la, _ la, la.

'Cause you know it's been a long time com-in', don't you let me fall, _

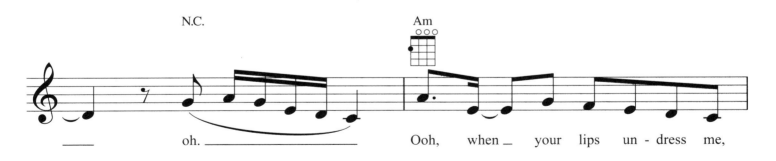

_ oh. _____ Ooh, when _ your lips un-dress me,

hooked on _ your tongue. Ooh, love, _ your kiss is dead-ly. Don't stop. I love it when you

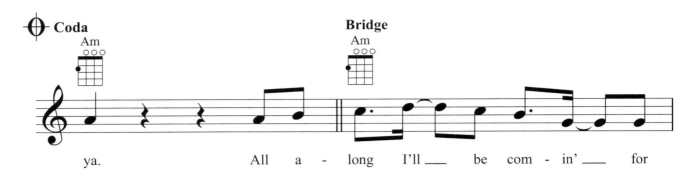

Coda

Bridge

ya.   All a - long I'll ___ be com - in' ___ for

ya.   And I hope it ___ meant some - thin' ___ to ya.   Call my

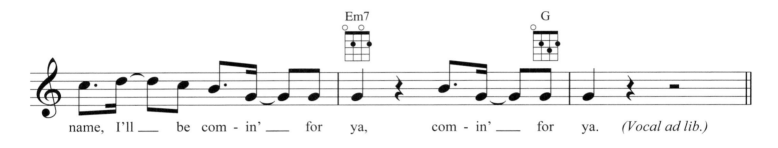

name, I'll ___ be com - in' ___ for ya,   com - in' ___ for ya.   *(Vocal ad lib.)*

Outro

(Instrumental)

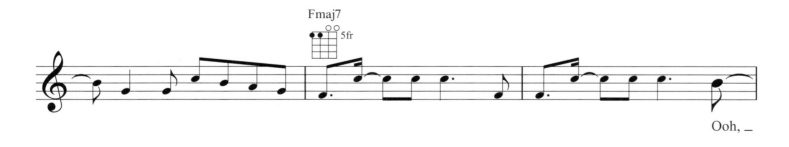

Ooh, _

___ I should be run - nin'.   Ooh, ___ you keep me com - in' ___ for ya.

Rolling in the Deep

Words and Music by Adele Adkins and Paul Epworth

your __ love re-mind me of _____ us. They keep me think-ing that we al-most had it

all. The scars of your _____ love, they leave me breath - less. I can't help

Chorus

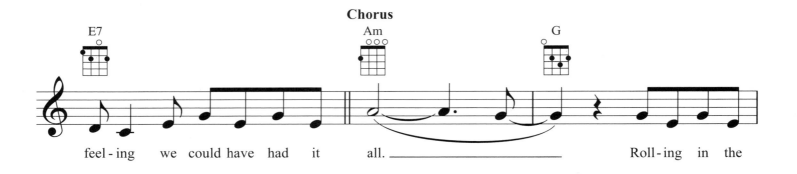

feel-ing we could have had it all. _____ Roll-ing in the

deep. _____ You had my heart in - side _____ of your hand, __

1.   *D.C.*
                                                                                                          (take 2nd ending)

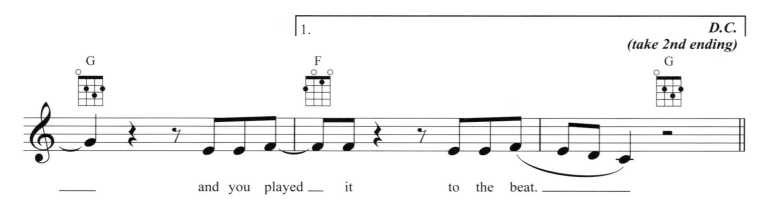

_____ and you played __ it to the beat. _____

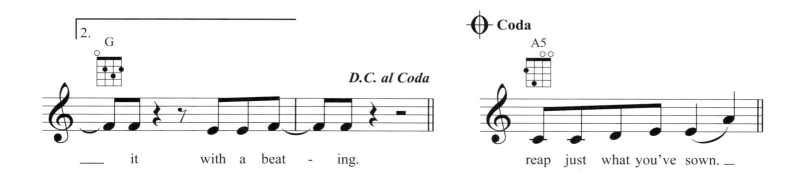

2. G — it with a beat - ing.

D.C. al Coda

Coda

A5 — reap just what you've sown. —

Outro

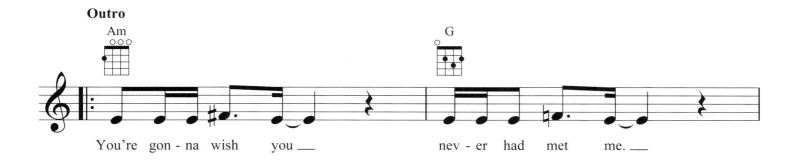

Am — You're gon - na wish you —

G — nev - er had met me. —

F — Tears are gon - na fall, —

G — roll - ing in the deep. —

Am

Additional Lyrics

2. See how I'll leave with every piece of you.
   Don't underestimate the things that I will do.
   There's a fire starting in my heart,
   Reaching a fever pitch and it's bringing me out the dark.

3. Baby, I have no story to be told,
   But I've heard one on you; now I'm gonna make your head burn.
   Think of me in the depths of your despair;
   Make a home down there, as mine sure won't be shared.

4. Throw your soul through every open door.
   Count your blessings to find what you look for.
   Turn my sorrows into treasured gold.
   You'll pay me back in kind and reap just what you've sown.

7 Years

Words and Music by Lukas Forchhammer, Morten Ristorp, Stefan Forrest,
David Labrel, Christopher Brown and Morten Pilegaard

Verse

Em   D   G   C

2. Once I was e-lev-en years old, my dad-dy told me, "Go get your-self a
3., 5. *See additional lyrics*

D   Em   D   G   Cmaj7

wife or you'll be lone-ly." _ Once I was e-lev-en years old.

Em   D   G

I al-ways had that dream __ like my dad-dy be-fore me,

C   D   Em   D

so I start-ed writ-ing songs, I start-ed writ-ing sto-ries. Some-thing a-bout that glo-ry

G   C   *To Coda* ⊕   D

just al-ways seemed to bore me, 'cause on-ly those I real-ly love will ev-er real-ly know me.

Verse

Em   D   G   C

4. Once I was twen-ty years old, my sto-ry got told, I was writ-ing 'bout ev-'ry-

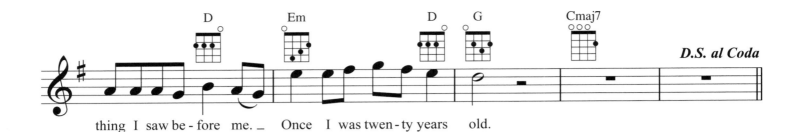

D.S. al Coda

thing I saw be - fore me. _ Once I was twen - ty years old.

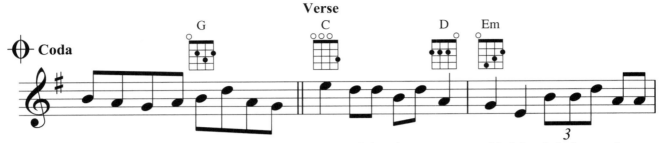

Coda

Verse

hind. My broth - er, I'm still sor - ry. 6. Soon I'll be six - ty years old. My dad - dy got six - ty-

one. Re - mem - ber life and then your life be - comes a bet - ter one. I made a man so hap - py

when I wrote a let - ter once. I hope my chil - dren come and vis - it once or twice a month.

Soon I'll be six - ty years old. Will I think the world is cold or will I have a lot of

chil - dren who can warm me? _ Soon I'll be six - ty years old.

190

Additional Lyrics

3. Once I was twenty years old, my story got told
   Before the morning sun, when life was lonely.
   Once I was twenty years old.
   I only see my goals, I don't believe in failure
   'Cause I know the smallest voices, they can make it major.
   I got my boys with me, at least those in favor,
   And if we don't meet before I leave, I hope I'll see you later.

5. Soon we'll be thirty years old. Our songs have been sold,
   We've travelled around the world and we're still roaming.
   Soon we'll be thirty years old.
   I'm still learning about life. My woman brought children for me
   So I can sing them all my songs and I can tell them stories.
   Most of my boys are with me, some are still out seeking glory
   And some I had to leave behind. My brother, I'm still sorry.

Shake It Off

Words and Music by Taylor Swift, Max Martin and Shellback

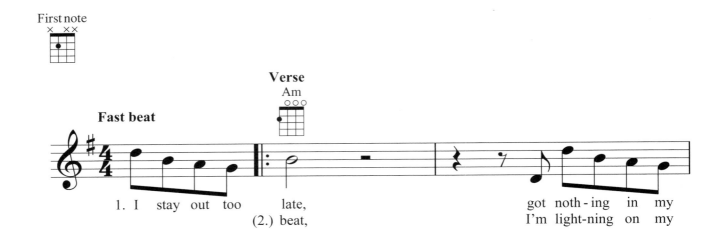

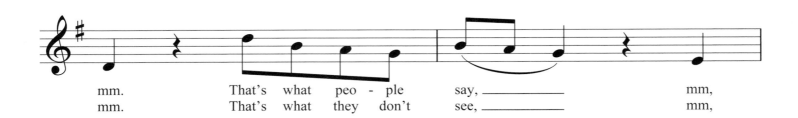

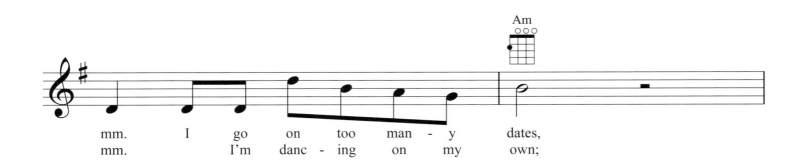

but I can't make 'em stay.
I make the moves up as I go.

At least, that's what people say, _____ mm,
And that's what they don't know, _____ mm,

mm. That's what peo - ple say, _____ mm, mm. But I keep
mm. That's what they don't know, _____ mm, mm. But I keep

Pre-Chorus

cruis - ing; can't stop, won't stop mov - ing. } It's
cruis - ing; can't stop, won't stop groov - ing. }

like I got this mu - sic in my mind say - ing,

"It's gon - na be al - right." _____ 'Cause the

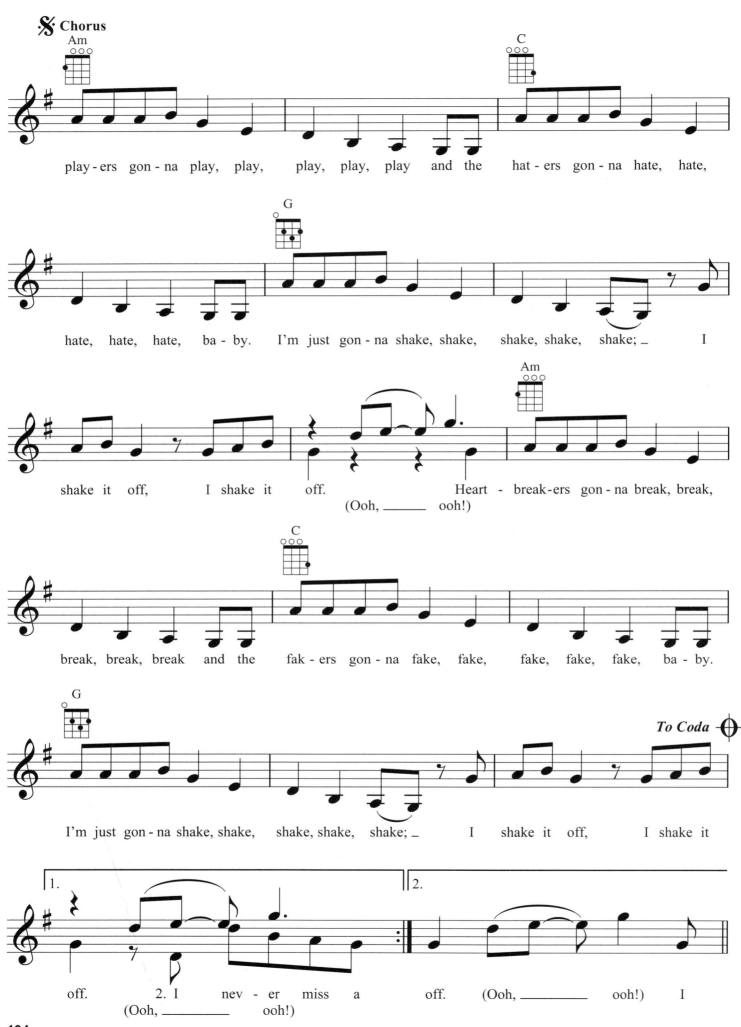

Bridge

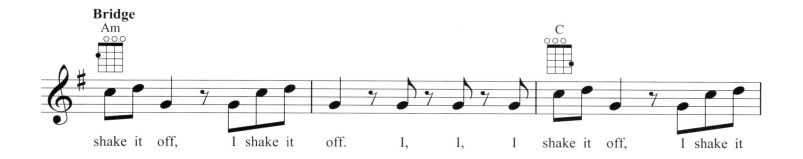

shake it off, I shake it off. I, I, I shake it off, I shake it

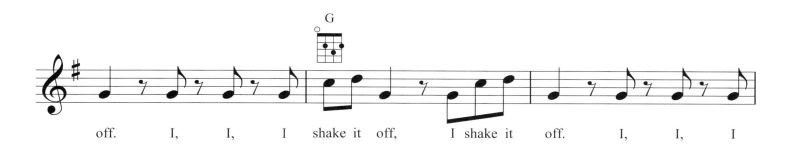

off. I, I, I shake it off, I shake it off. I, I, I

shake it off, I shake it off. _____

(Ooh, _____ ooh!)

Interlude

1. *Spoken: (See additional lyrics)*
2. *Rap: (See additional lyrics)*

D.S. al Coda

Rap ends   Yeah, _____ oh. _____ 'Cause the

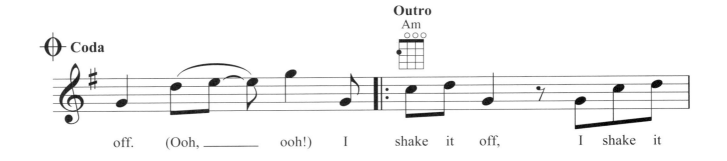

off. (Ooh, _____ ooh!) I shake it off, I shake it

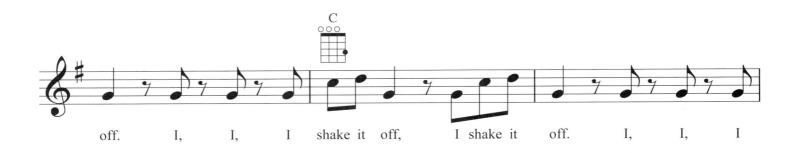

off. I, I, I shake it off, I shake it off. I, I, I

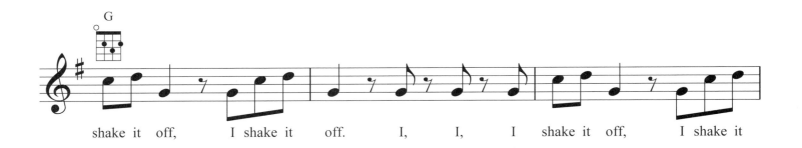

shake it off, I shake it off. I, I, I shake it off, I shake it

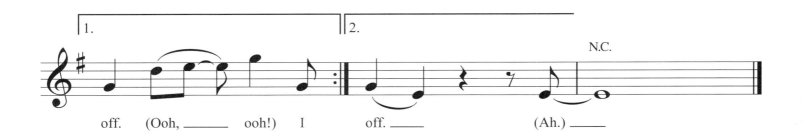

1. off. (Ooh, _____ ooh!) I 2. off. _____ (Ah.) _____

Additional Lyrics

Spoken: Hey, hey, hey! Just think: While you've been gettin'
Down and out about the liars and the dirty, dirty cheats of the world,
You could've been gettin' down to this sick beat!

Rap: My ex-man brought his new girlfriend.
She's like, "Oh, my god!" But I'm just gonna shake.
And to the fella over there with the hella good hair,
Won't you come on over, baby? We can shake, shake, shake.

Royals

Words and Music by Ella Yelich-O'Connor and Joel Little

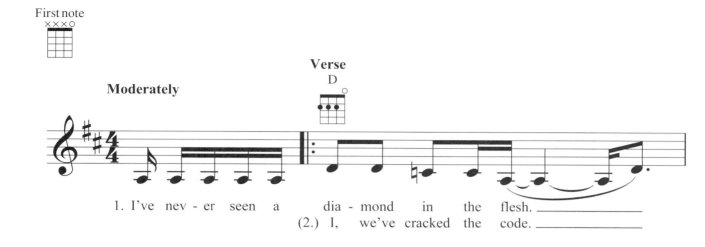

1. I've nev-er seen a dia-mond in the flesh. _____
(2.) I, we've cracked the code. _____

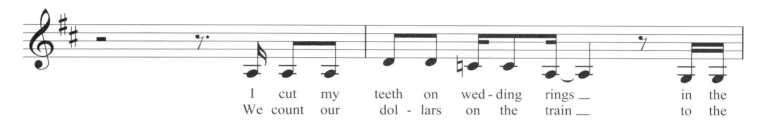

I cut my teeth on wed-ding rings _____ in the
We count our dol-lars on the train _____ to the

mov-ies. _____ And I'm not proud of my ad-dress. _____
par-ty. _____ And ev-'ry-one who knows us knows _____

In the torn-up town, no post-code
that we're fine with this. We did-n't come from

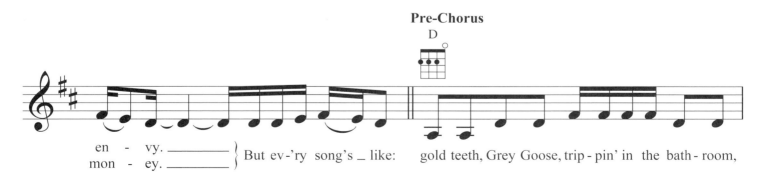

en-vy. _____ } But ev-'ry song's _ like: gold teeth, Grey Goose, trip-pin' in the bath-room,
mon-ey. _____

blood stains, ball gowns, trash-in' the ho-tel room. We don't care, __ we're driv-in'

Cad-il-lacs in our dreams. _ But ev-'ry-bod-y's like: Cris-tal, May-bach, dia-monds on your time-piece,

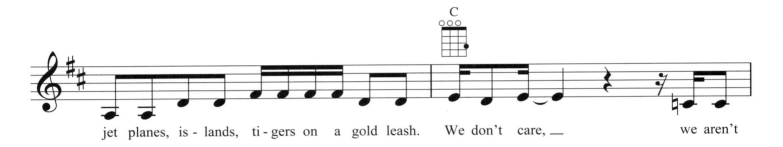

jet planes, is-lands, ti-gers on a gold leash. We don't care, __ we aren't

𝄋 **Chorus**

caught up in your love af-fair. __ And we'll nev-er be roy-als, (roy-als.)

It don't run in our _ blood. __ That kind of luxe just ain't _ for us. __ We crave a

dif-f'rent kind _ of buzz. __ Let me be __ your rul-er, (rul-er.)

Shallow

from A STAR IS BORN

Words and Music by Stefani Germanotta, Mark Ronson, Andrew Wyatt and Anthony Rossomando

* *Male vocal written at sung pitch.*

for change, ___ and in the bad times I

1.

fear my - self. ___

2.

fear my - self. ___

Chorus

I'm off the deep ___ end. Watch as I dive ___ in:

I'll nev - er meet ___ the ground. _____ Crash through the sur - face,

where they can't hurt ___ us. We're far from the shal - low now. ___

Shape of You

**Words and Music by Ed Sheeran, Kevin Briggs, Kandi Burruss,
Tameka Cottle, Steve Mac and Johnny McDaid**

Chorus

I'm in love with the shape of you. We push and pull like a mag-net

do. Al-though my heart is fall-ing, too, I'm in love with your bod - y.

Last night you were in my room, and now my bed-sheets smell like

you. Ev-'ry day dis-cov-er-ing some-thing brand - new. Well, I'm in love with your bod - y.

(Oh, I, oh, I, oh, I, oh, I.) Well, I'm in love with your bod - y.

(Oh, I, oh, I, oh, I, oh, I.) Well, I'm in love with your bod - y.

(Oh, I, oh, I, oh, I, oh, I.) Well, I'm in love with your bod - y. ___

___ Ev-'ry day dis-cov-er-ing some-thing brand - new. I'm in love with the shape of

Verse

you.
2. One week in, ___ we let the sto - ry be - gin, ___ we're go - ing

out on our first date. ___ You and me are thrift - y, so go "all you can eat," ___ fill up your

bag and I fill up a plate. We talk for hours and hours ___ a-bout sweet and the sour, ___ and how your

fam-i-ly's do-ing o-kay, and leave and get in a tax - i, then kiss in the back ___ seat 'til the

207

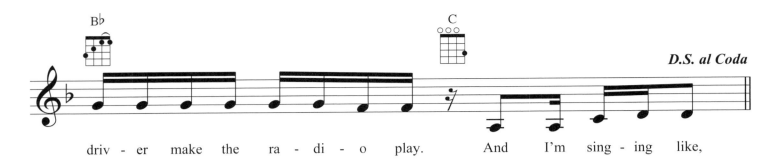

Bb   C   *D.S. al Coda*

driv - er make the ra - di - o play.   And   I'm   sing - ing   like,

Interlude

N.C.

⊕ **Coda**

you. Come on, ___ be my ba - by, come on.   Come on, ___ be my ba - by, come on.

Come on, ___ be my ba - by, come on.   Come on, ___ be my ba - by, come on.

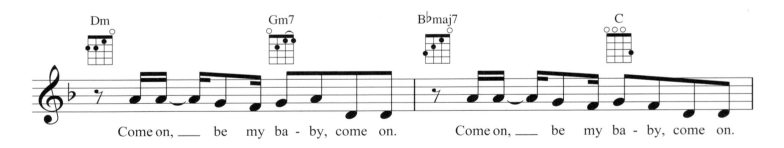

Dm   Gm7   Bbmaj7   C

Come on, ___ be my ba - by, come on.   Come on, ___ be my ba - by, come on.

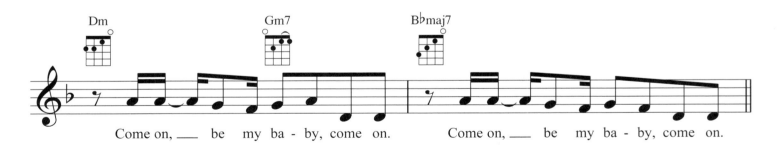

Dm   Gm7   Bbmaj7

Come on, ___ be my ba - by, come on.   Come on, ___ be my ba - by, come on.

Outro-Chorus

Dm   Gm   Bb   Csus4   C

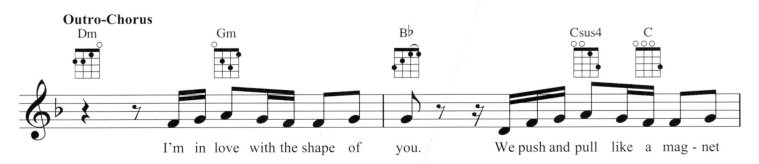

I'm in love with the shape of you.   We push and pull like a mag - net

Some Nights

Words and Music by Jeff Bhasker, Andrew Dost, Jack Antonoff and Nate Ruess

211

al - ways win. But I still wake __ up, _____ I still

see your __ ghost. __ Oh, Lord, I'm still not __ sure _____ what I

stand for, __ oh. __ Whoa, _____ what do I stand for? _ What do I stand for? _

Most nights, _ I _____ don't know. _____ Oh, come on. __

Bridge 1

(Spoken:) So this is it.   I sold my soul for this?   _Washed my hands of that for this?_

Ooh, na, __ na.

Ooh, na, __ na, come on. _____   Ooh, na, __ na, come on. _
I miss my mom and dad for this?   _No, when I see stars, when I see, when I see stars, that's all they are._

214

When I hear songs...

Verse

215

Bridge 2

break-ing for ___ my sis - ter _____ and the con that she ___ called "love." ___   When I

look in - to ___ my neph - ew's eyes, _____   man, you would-n't be - lieve ___

the most a - maz - ing things   that can come   from _____

___   some ter - ri - ble

Interlude

lies. _____

Ah, _____

ah, _____

ah, _____ ah. _____

Outro-Verse

Coda

The oth - er night, you would - n't be - lieve the dream _____

_____ I just had a - bout _____ you and me. I called you up, but we both a - gree.

It's for the best you did - n't lis - ten. _____

It's for the best we get _____ our dis - tance, _____ oh. _____

217

Someone You Loved

Words and Music by Lewis Capaldi, Benjamin Kohn, Peter Kelleher, Thomas Barnes and Samuel Roman

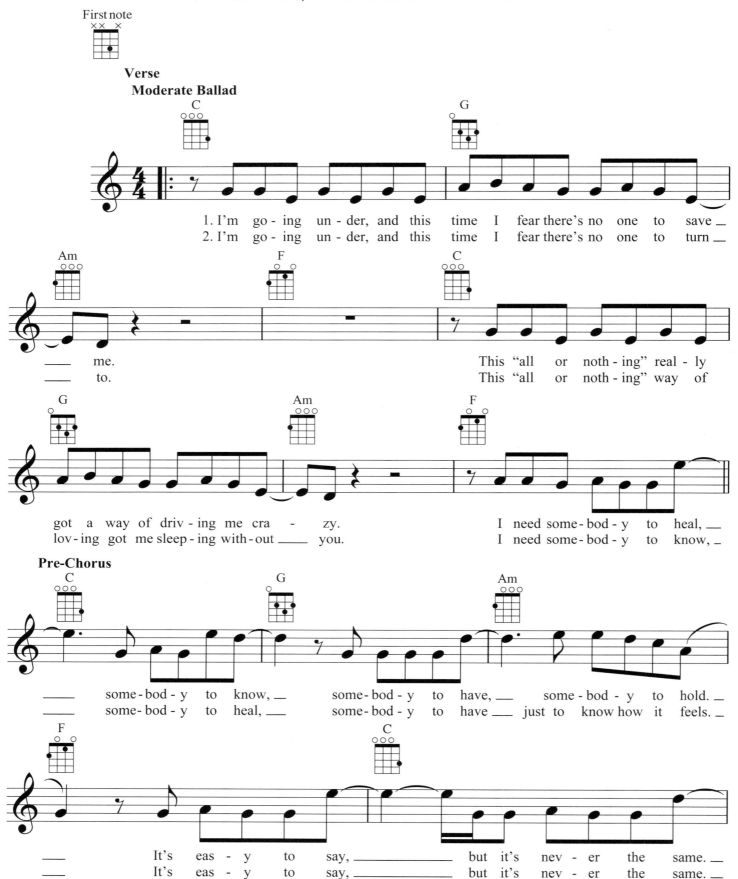

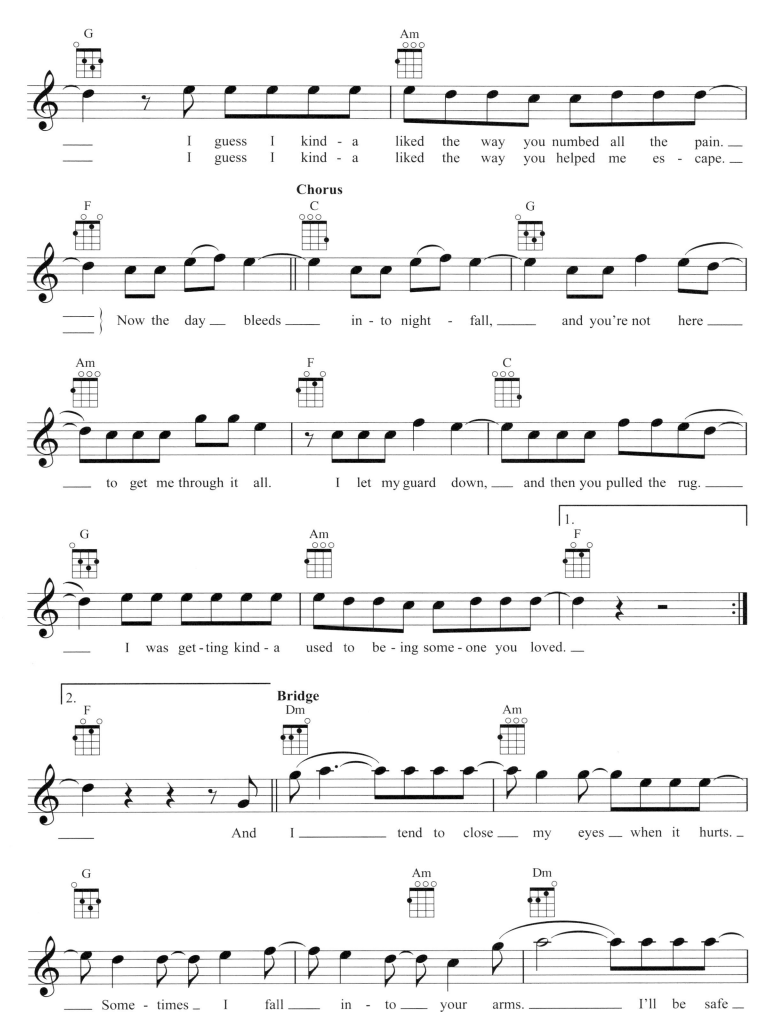

I guess I kind-a liked the way you numbed all the pain. __
I guess I kind-a liked the way you helped me es-cape. __

Chorus

__ } Now the day __ bleeds __ in-to night-fall, _____ and you're not here _____

__ to get me through it all. I let my guard down, __ and then you pulled the rug. _____

1.

__ I was get-ting kind-a used to be-ing some-one you loved. __

2.

Bridge

__ And I _____ tend to close __ my eyes __ when it hurts. __

__ Some-times __ I fall __ in-to __ your arms. _____ I'll be safe __

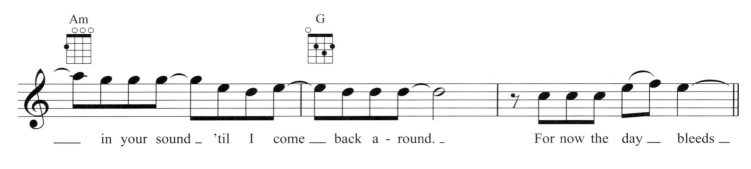

_____ in your sound _ 'til I come _ back a - round. _ For now the day _ bleeds _

Chorus

_____ in - to night - fall, _____ and you're not here _____ to get me through it all.

I let my guard down, ___ and then you pulled the rug. _____ I was get - ting kind - a

used to be - ing some-one you loved. _ But now the day _ bleeds _ ___ I let my guard down, _

Outro

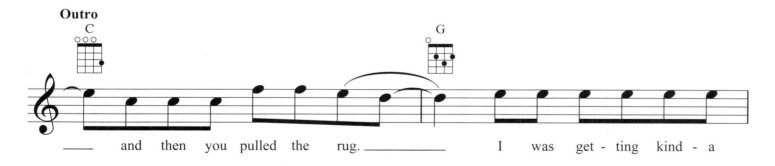

_____ and then you pulled the rug. _____ I was get - ting kind - a

used to be - ing some-one you loved. ___

Stay with Me

Words and Music by Sam Smith, James Napier, William Edward Phillips, Tom Petty and Jeff Lynne

1. Guess it's true, I'm not good at a one-night stand.
2. Why am I so e-mo-tion-al?

But I still need love 'cause I'm just a man.
No, it's not a good look. Gain some self-con-trol.

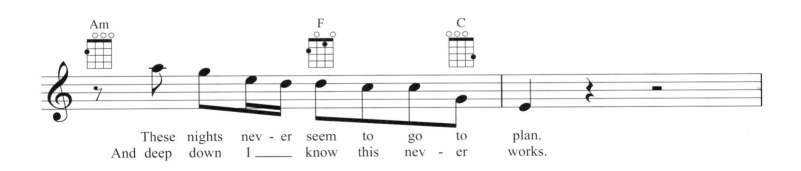

These nights nev-er seem to go to plan.
And deep down I ___ know this nev-er works.

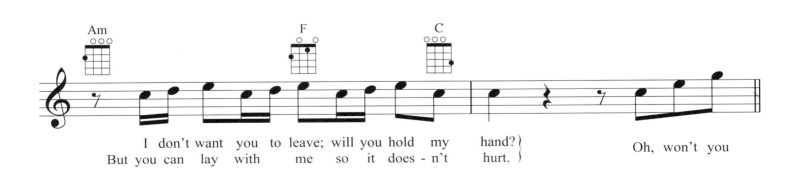

I don't want you to leave; will you hold my hand?
But you can lay with me so it does-n't hurt.

Oh, won't you

stay ___ with me? ___ 'Cause you're all ___ I need. ___

___ This ain't ___ love, it's clear ___ to see. ___

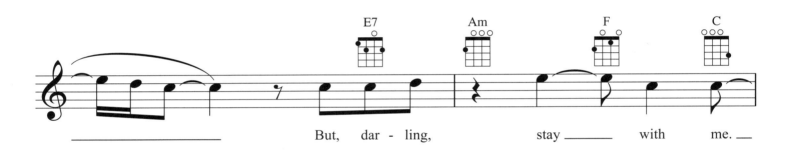

___ But, dar - ling, stay ___ with me. ___

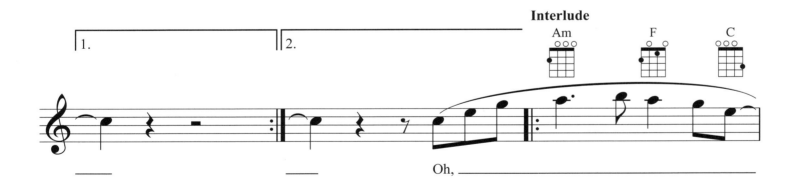

___ ___ Oh, _____

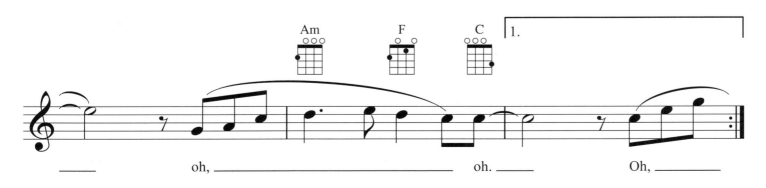

___ oh, _____ oh. ___ Oh, ___

Outro-Chorus

Oh, won't you stay _____ with me? _____

_____ 'Cause you're all _____ I need. _____

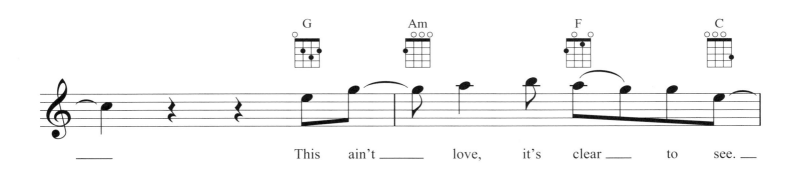

_____ This ain't _____ love, it's clear _____ to see. _____

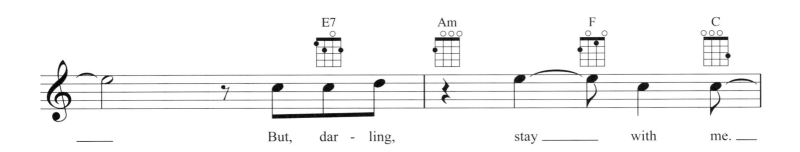

_____ But, dar - ling, stay _____ with me. _____

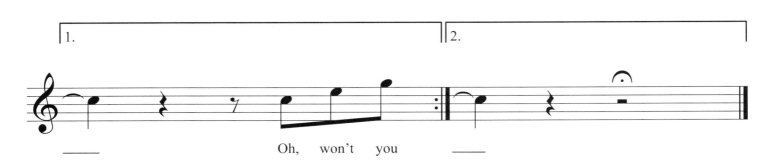

_____ Oh, won't you _____

223

Something Just Like This

Words and Music by Andrew Taggart, Chris Martin, Guy Berryman, Jonny Buckland and Will Champion

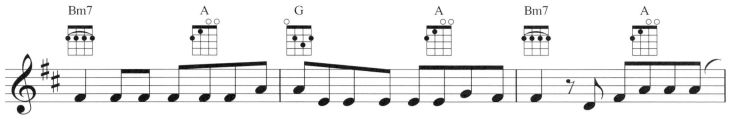

risk? I'm not look-ing for some-bod-y with some su-per-hu-man gifts, some su-per-he-ro, __

To Coda

__ some fair-y-tale __ bliss. Just some-thing I can turn to, some-bod-y I can

Chorus

kiss. I want some-thing just like __ this. Do do do do do do, __ do do do do, __

__ do do do do do do. Oh, I want some-thing just like __

__ this. Do do do do do do, __ do do do do, __ do do do do do do.

Oh, I want some-thing just like __ this.

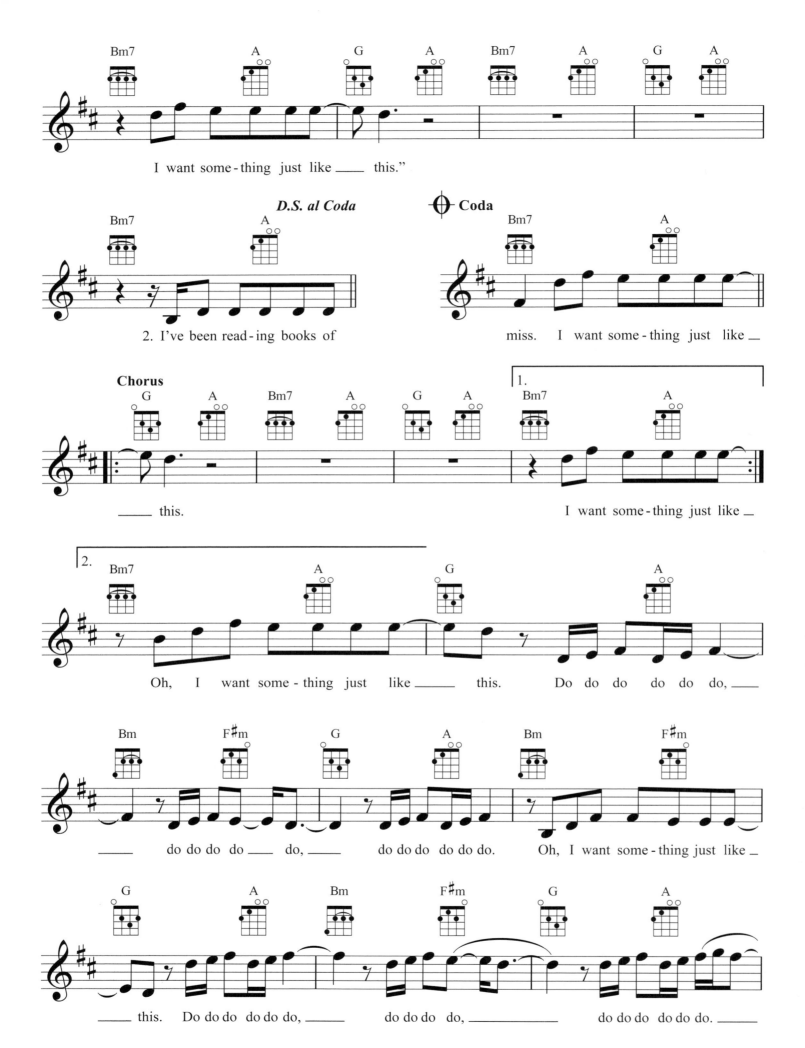

I want some-thing just like _____ this."

D.S. al Coda

Coda

2. I've been read-ing books of

miss. I want some-thing just like _

Chorus

_____ this.

1.

I want some-thing just like _

2.

Oh, I want some-thing just like _____ this. Do do do do do do, _____

_____ do do do do _____ do, _____ do do do do do do. Oh, I want some-thing just like _

_____ this. Do do do do do do, _____ do do do do, _____ do do do do do do.

Outro

Where d'you wan-na go? _ How much you wan-na risk? I'm not look-ing for some-

bod-y with some su-per-hu-man gifts, some su-per-he-ro, ____ some fair-y-tale _

bliss. Just some-thing I can turn to, some-bod-y I can kiss. I want some-thing just like _

____ this.

Oh, I want some-thing just like ____ this.

Stitches

Words and Music by Teddy Geiger, Danny Parker and Daniel Kyriakides

Pre-Chorus

_____ on my _____ own.

Got a feel-ing that I'm go-in' un-der, but I know that I'll make it out a-live _____ if I quit call-ing you my lov-er and move on. _____

Chorus

You watch me bleed un-til I can't _____ breathe, shak-ing, fall-ing on-to my _____ knees. And now that I'm with-out _____ your kiss-es, _____ I'll be need-ing stitch-es. _____

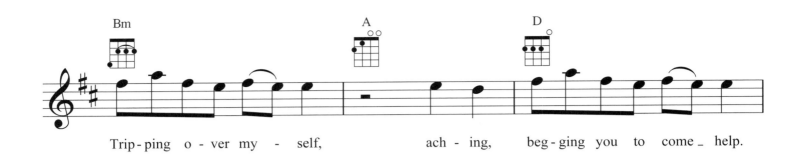

Trip-ping o-ver my-self, ach-ing, beg-ging you to come _ help.

And now that I'm with-out _ your kiss - es, _

To Coda ⊕   **Interlude**

I'll be need - ing stitch - es. _

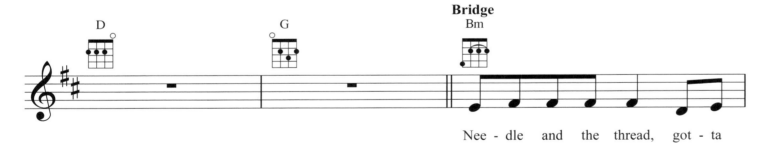

Bridge

Nee - dle and the thread, got - ta

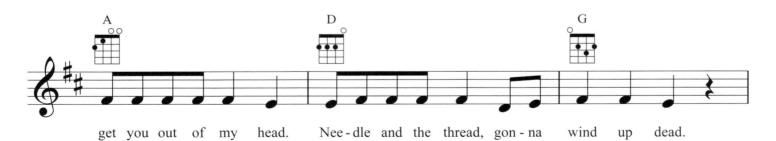

get you out of my head. Nee - dle and the thread, gon - na wind up dead.

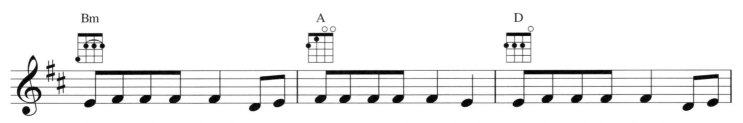

Nee - dle and the thread, got - ta get you out of my head. Nee - dle and the thread, gon - na

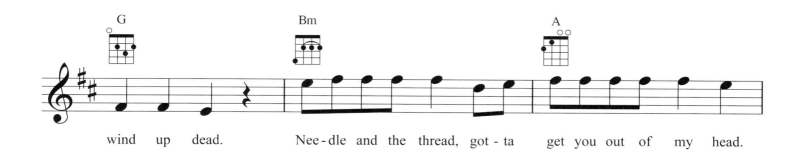

wind up dead.   Nee-dle and the thread, got-ta   get you out of my head.

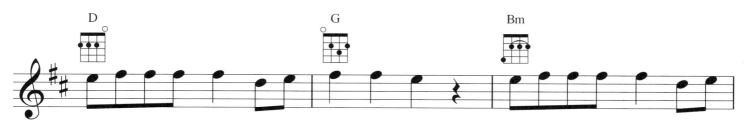

Nee-dle and the thread, gon-na   wind up dead.   Nee-dle and the thread, got-ta

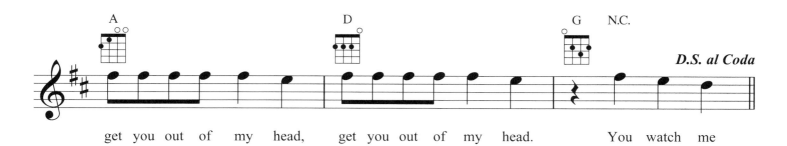

D.S. al Coda

get you out of my head,   get you out of my head.   You watch me

Coda

Outro

- es. Now that   I'm with-out ___ your kiss   -   es, ___

I'll be need - ing stitch - es. Now that   I'm with - out ___ your kiss -

- es, ___   I'll be need - ing stitch - es. ___

Take Me to Church

Words and Music by Andrew Hozier-Byrne

Verse
Moderate Ballad

1. My lov-er's got hu-mor. She's the gig-gle at a fu-n'ral.

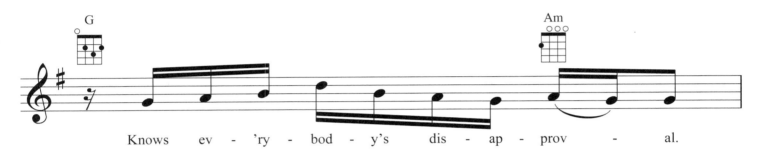

Knows ev-'ry-bod-y's dis-ap-prov-al.

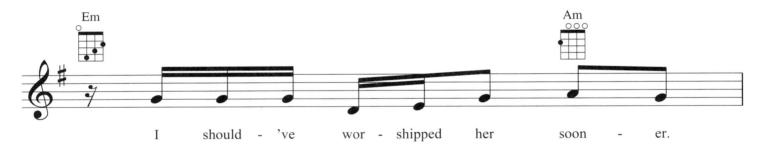

I should-'ve wor-shipped her soon-er.

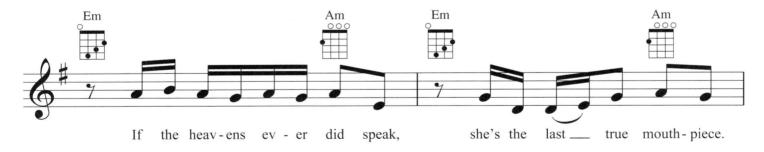

If the heav-ens ev-er did speak, she's the last ___ true mouth-piece.

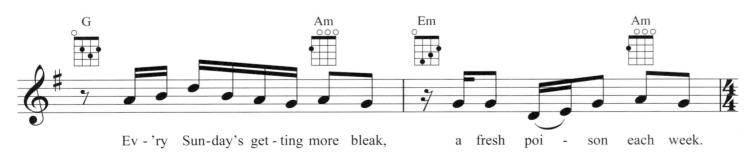

Ev-'ry Sun-day's get-ting more bleak, a fresh poi-son each week.

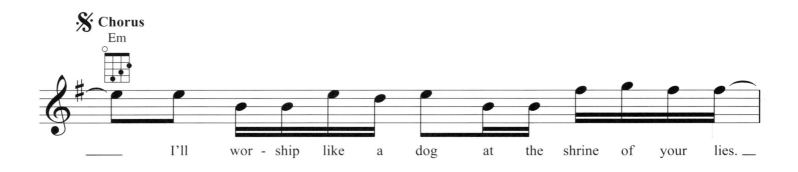

Em

____ I'll wor - ship like a dog at the shrine of your lies. _

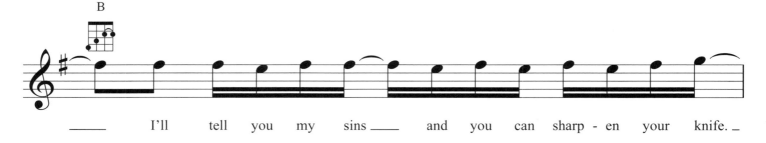

B

____ I'll tell you my sins ____ and you can sharp - en your knife. _

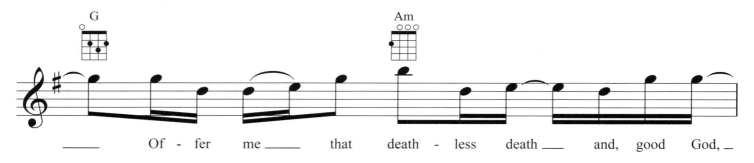

G   Am

____ Of - fer me ____ that death - less death ___ and, good God, _

Em

____ let me give you my life. Take me to church, _

____ I'll wor - ship like a dog at the shrine of your lies, _

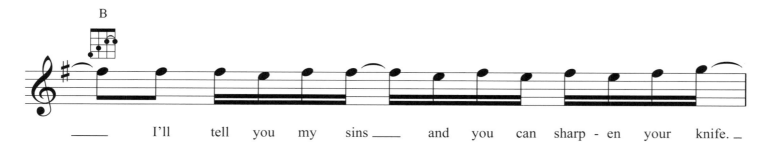

B

____ I'll tell you my sins ____ and you can sharp - en your knife. _

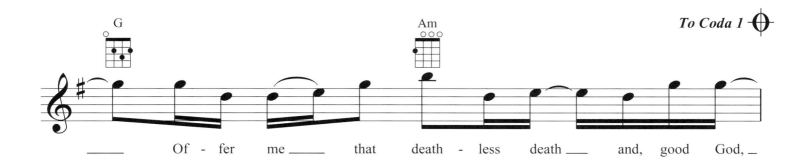

_Of - fer me ____ that death - less death ____ and, good God, _____

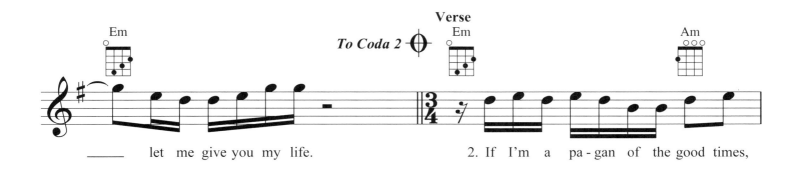

_____ let me give you my life.   2. If I'm a pa-gan of the good times,

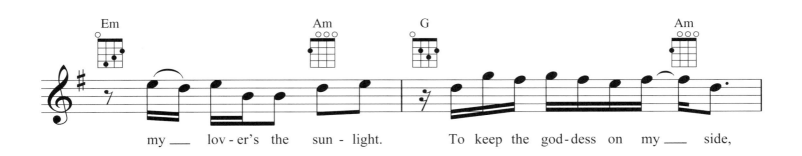

my ____ lov-er's the sun - light.   To keep the god-dess on my ____ side,

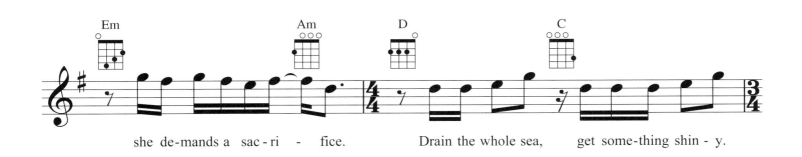

she de-mands a sac-ri - fice.   Drain the whole sea,   get some-thing shin-y.

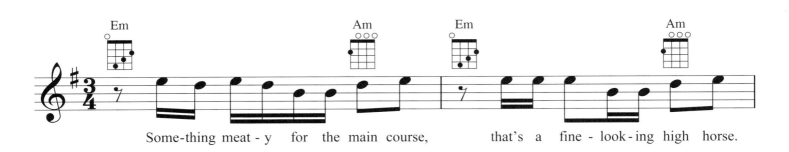

Some-thing meat-y for the main course,   that's a fine-look-ing high horse.

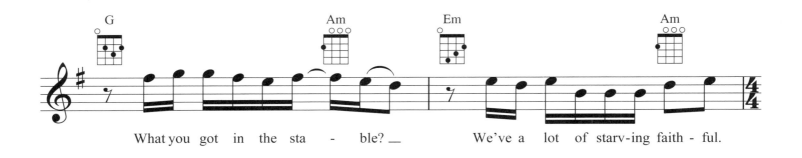

What you got in the sta - ble? __ We've a lot of starv-ing faith - ful.

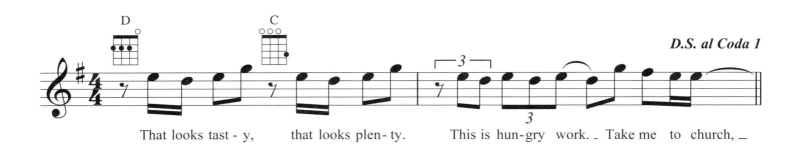

D.S. al Coda 1

That looks tast - y, that looks plen - ty. This is hun-gry work. _ Take me to church, __

Coda 1

__ let me give you my life.

Bridge

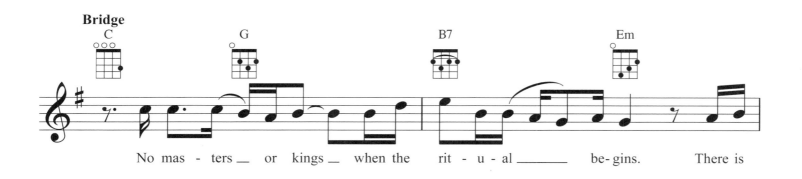

No mas - ters __ or kings __ when the rit - u - al _____ be - gins. There is

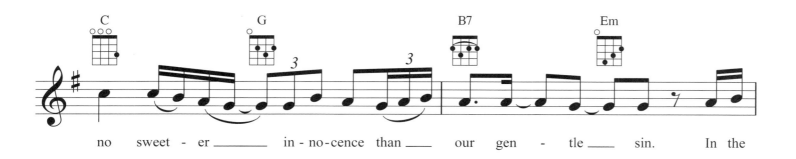

no sweet - er _____ in - no-cence than ___ our gen - tle ___ sin. In the

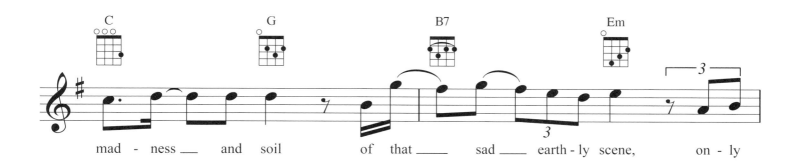

mad - ness __ and soil of that __ sad __ earth-ly scene, on - ly

then I __ am __ hu - man, on - ly then I __ am __

Pre-Chorus

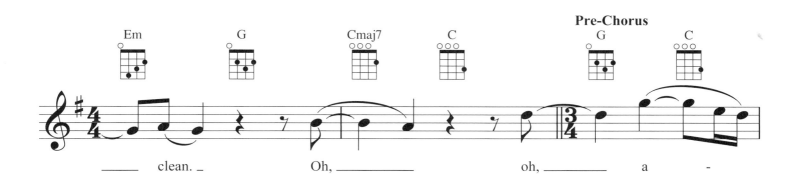

__ clean. _ Oh, __ oh, __ a -

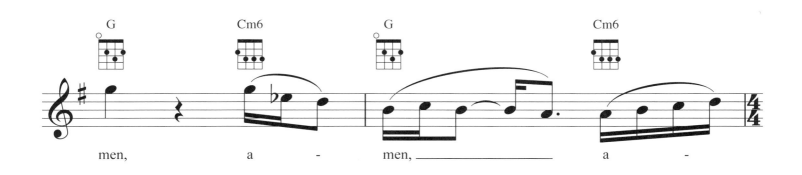

men, a - men, __ a -

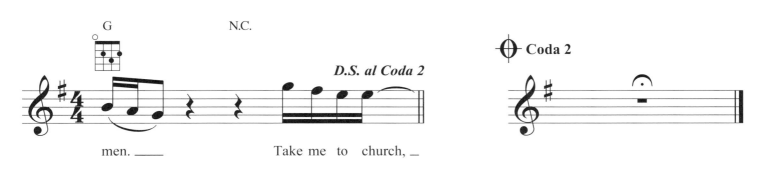

men. __ Take me to church, _

237

Tear in My Heart

Words and Music by Tyler Joseph

But that's o - kay, I'll just a - void the holes so you sleep fine.

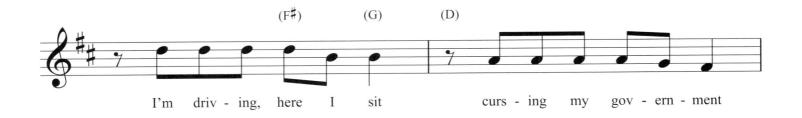

I'm driv - ing, here I sit cur - sing my gov - ern - ment

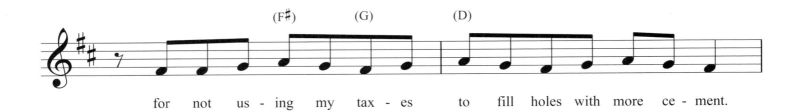

for not us - ing my tax - es to fill holes with more ce - ment.

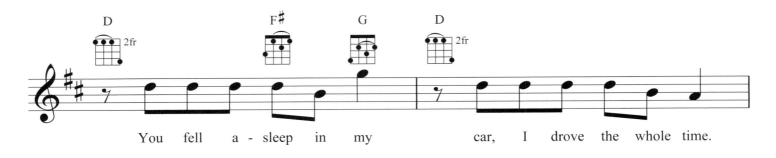

You fell a - sleep in my car, I drove the whole time.

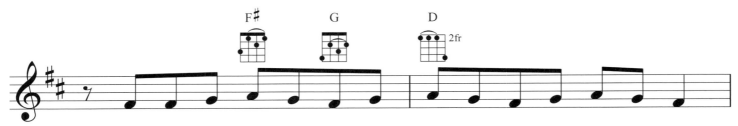

But that's o - kay, I'll just a - void the holes so you sleep fine.

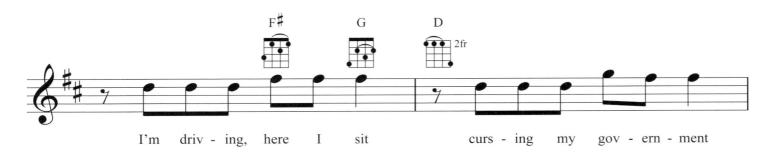

I'm driv - ing, here I sit cur - sing my gov - ern - ment

for not us - ing my tax - es to fill holes with more ce - ment.

Verse
Straight 8ths

*Let chord ring.

3. Some - times you got - ta bleed to know, oh, ___ oh,

that you're a - live and have a soul - oul - oul. But it takes some - one to come a -

Chorus

round to show you how. ___ She's the tear in my ___ heart, I'm a - live. ___

___ She's the tear in my ___ heart, I'm on fi - re. She's the tear in my ___

Outro-Chorus

heart, take me high - er than I've ev - er been. ___ My heart is my ar -

mor. She's the tear in my __ heart, she's a carv - er. She's a butch-er with a

smile, cut me far - ther than I've ev - er been, __

than I've ev - er been, _____ than I've ev - er been, __

oh, _____ than I've ev - er been. __ My heart is my ar -
*Let chord ring.

mor. She's the tear in my heart, she's a carv - er. She's a butch-er with a

Slower, with freedom

smile, cut me far - ther than I've ev - er been.

Walk Me Home

Words and Music by Alecia Moore, Scott Harris and Nate Ruess

know it's get - ting late, so what do you say we leave this
show me how we're good. I think that we could do some

𝄋 **Chorus**

place? _ Walk me home _ in the dead of night.
good. _

I can't be ___ a - lone with all that's on my mind. So,

To Coda ⊕

say you'll stay _ with me to - night. 'Cause there is so much wrong

1.
go - ing on ___ out - side. 3. There's

2. **Interlude**

Ooh. _____ Ooh. _____

side.

Tennessee Whiskey

Words and Music by Dean Dillon and Linda Hargrove

First note

Verse
Slowly, in 4

1. Used to spend my nights _ out   in bar - rooms.

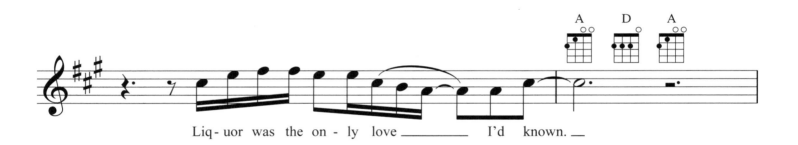

Liq - uor was the on - ly love _____ I'd   known. _

But you res - cued me _ from reach - in' for the bot - tom ____   and brought _ me

back ____ from be-in' ____ too far gone. ____ You're_ as

𝄋 Chorus

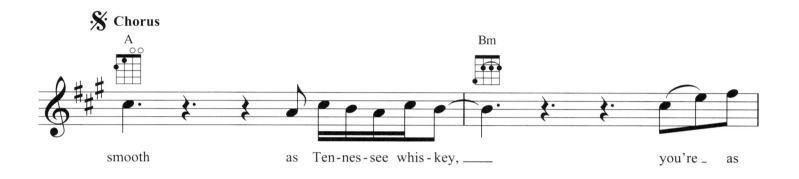

smooth as Ten-nes-see whis-key, ____ you're_ as

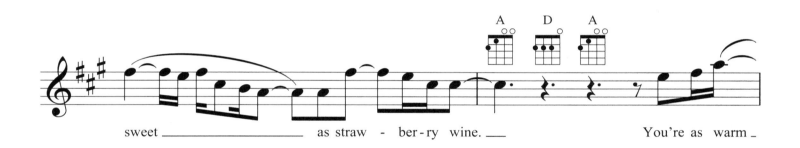

sweet _____ as straw - ber-ry wine. __ You're as warm_

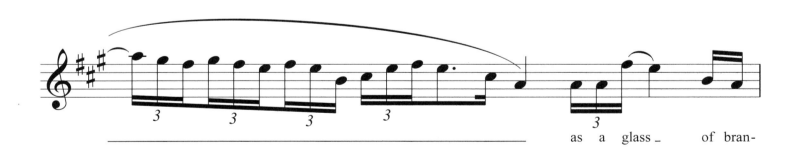

_____ as a glass_ of bran-

To Coda 2 ⊕

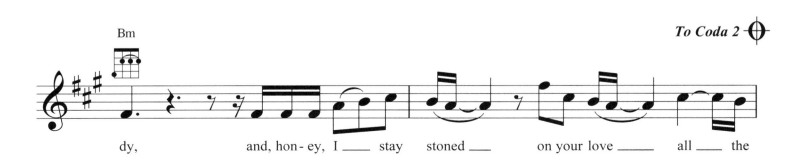

dy, and, hon- ey, I ___ stay stoned ___ on your love ___ all ___ the

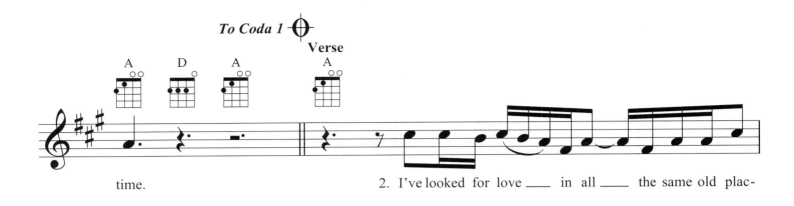

time.

2. I've looked for love ___ in all ___ the same old plac-

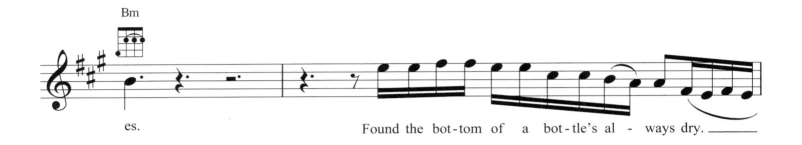

es.

Found the bot-tom of a bot-tle's al - ways dry. _____

_____

But when you poured _ out your heart, _ I did-n't waste

it,

'cause there's noth - in' _____ like your love _____ to get me high. _

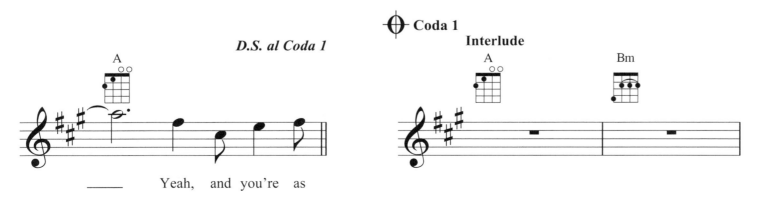

_____ Yeah, and you're as

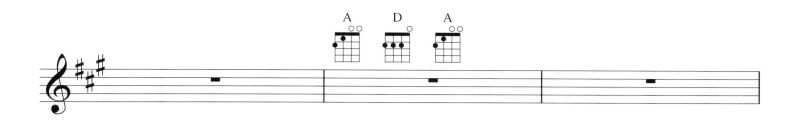

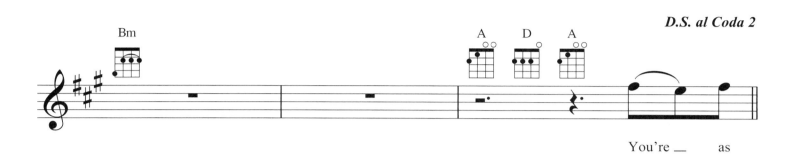

D.S. al Coda 2

You're ___ as

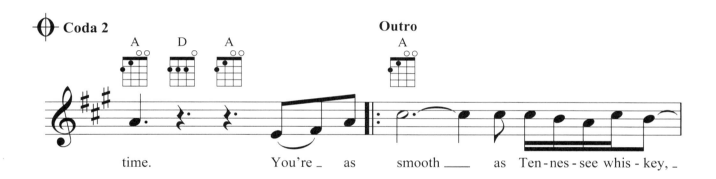

Coda 2   **Outro**

time.   You're ___ as   smooth ____ as Ten-nes-see whis-key, __

___   Ten-nes-see whis-key, ___   Ten-nes-see whis-key. __

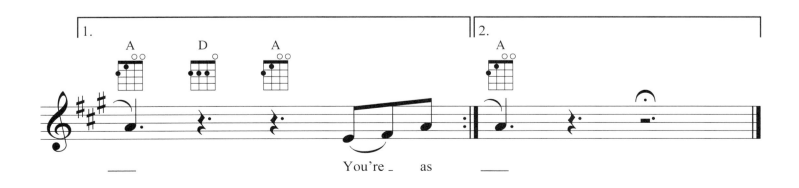

1.   2.

___   You're ___ as ___

Thinking Out Loud

Words and Music by Ed Sheeran and Amy Wadge

First note

Verse
Moderately

1. When your legs don't work like they used to be - fore
2. When my hair's all but gone and my mem - o - ry fades

and I can't sweep you off of your feet,
and the crowds don't re - mem - ber my name,

will your mouth still re - mem - ber the taste of my love?
when my hands don't _ play the _ strings the same way,

Will your eyes still smile from your cheeks? And, dar - ling, I
I know you will still love me the same. 'Cause, hon - ey, your

will __ be lov - ing you | till __ we're sev - en - ty. ____
soul __ could nev - er grow | old; __ it's ev - er - green. __

____
____

And, ba - by, my
And, ba - by, your

heart __ could still feel as | hard __ at twen - ty - three. __
smile's _ for - ev - er in | my mind __ and mem - o - ry. __

_____
_____

And I'm think - ing 'bout how ____
And I'm think - ing 'bout how ____

Pre-Chorus

peo - ple fall in love in mys - te - ri - ous ways, ____
peo - ple fall in love in mys - te - ri - ous ways, ____ and

may - be just the touch of a hand. ____ Well,
may - be it's all part of a plan. ____ Well,

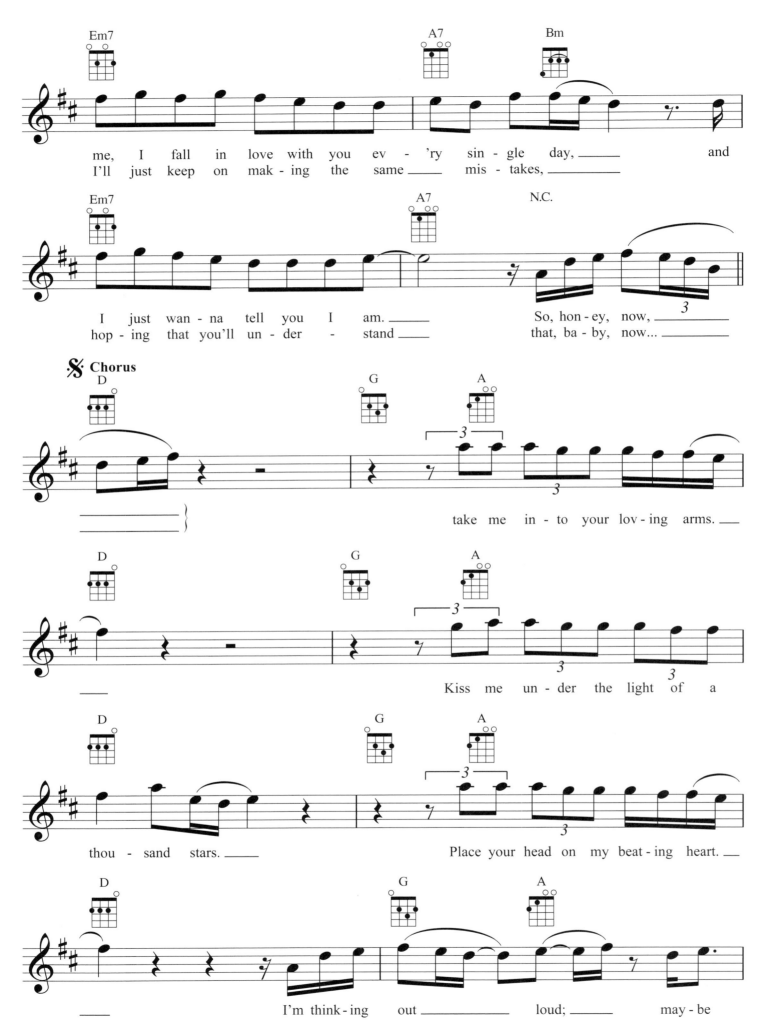

me, I fall in love with you ev - 'ry sin - gle day, _____ and
I'll just keep on mak - ing the same _____ mis - takes, _____

I just wan - na tell you I am. _____ So, hon - ey, now, _____
hop - ing that you'll un - der - stand _____ that, ba - by, now... _____

𝄋 Chorus

take me in - to your lov - ing arms. _____

Kiss me un - der the light of a

thou - sand stars. _____ Place your head on my beat - ing heart. _____

I'm think - ing out _____ loud; _____ may - be

we found love right where we are. where we are.

Interlude

(La, la,

la, la, la, la, la, la, la, la, la, la, la.)

D.S. al Coda

So, ba-by, now, —

Coda

where we are. Ba-by,

Outro

we found love right where we are. _____ And

we found love right where we are. _____

This Town

**Words and Music by Niall Horan, Michael Needle,
Daniel Bryer and Jamie Scott**

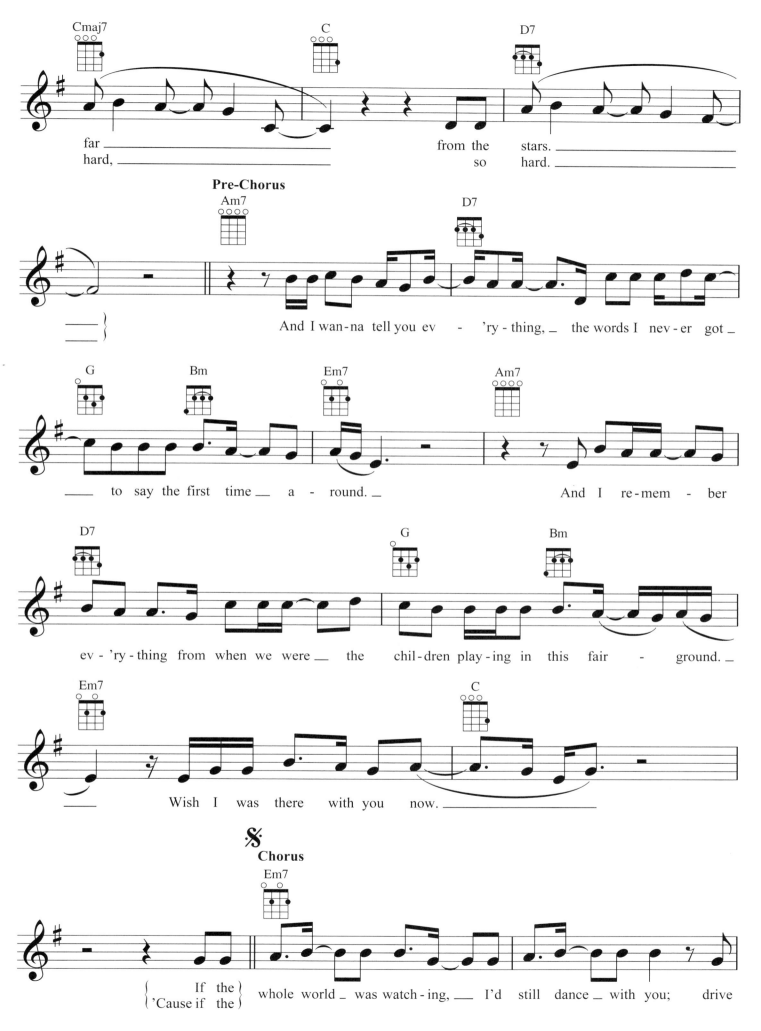

far _____
hard, _____

from the   stars. _____

so   hard. _____

Pre-Chorus

And I wan-na tell you ev - 'ry-thing, _ the words I nev-er got _

____ to say the first time _ a - round. _   And I re-mem - ber

ev - 'ry-thing from when we were _ the   chil-dren play-ing in this fair - ground. _

____   Wish I was there with you now. _____

Chorus

{ If the }
{ 'Cause if the }   whole world _ was watch-ing, ___ I'd still dance _ with you;   drive

high - ways _ and by - ways _ to   be   there _ with you.   O - ver _ and o - ver, _ the

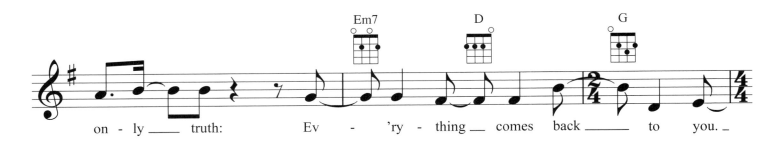

on - ly ___ truth: Ev - 'ry - thing _ comes back ____ to   you. _

1.

_   Mm. _____   3. I

2., 3.   **Chorus 2**

_   You   still make _ me nerv - ous _ when you   walk   in the room. _   Them

but - ter - flies, _   they   come a - live ___ when   I'm   next _ to you.

O - ver _   and   o - ver, _ the   on - ly ____ truth: Ev -

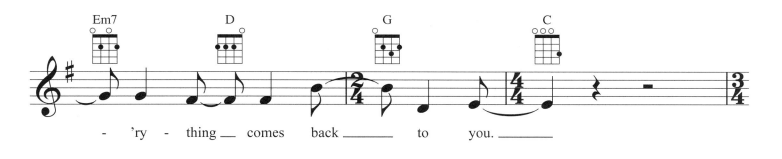

-'ry - thing ___ comes back _____ to you. _____

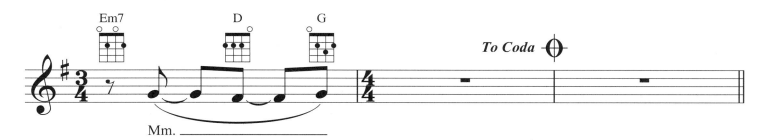

To Coda ⊕

Mm. _____

Bridge

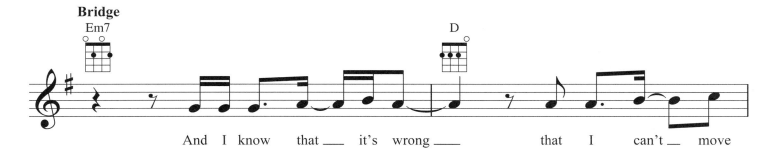

And I know that ___ it's wrong ___ that I can't ___ move

D.S. al Coda
(take 2nd ending)

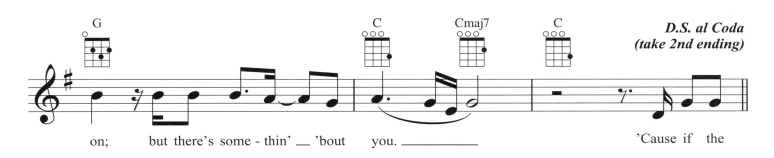

on; but there's some - thin' ___ 'bout you. _____ 'Cause if the

Outro

⊕ **Coda**

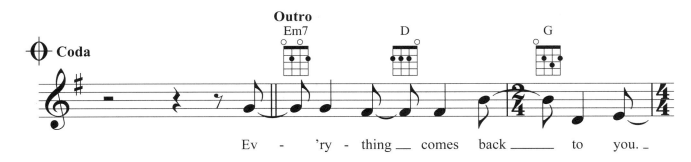

Ev - 'ry - thing ___ comes back _____ to you. __

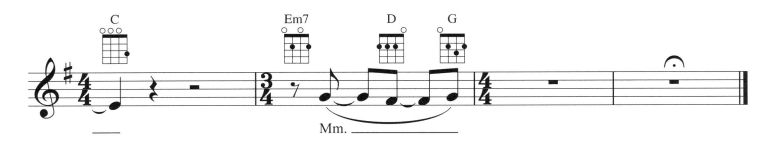

___ Mm. _____

257

A Thousand Years

from the Summit Entertainment film THE TWILIGHT SAGA: BREAKING DAWN – PART 1
Words and Music by David Hodges and Christina Perri

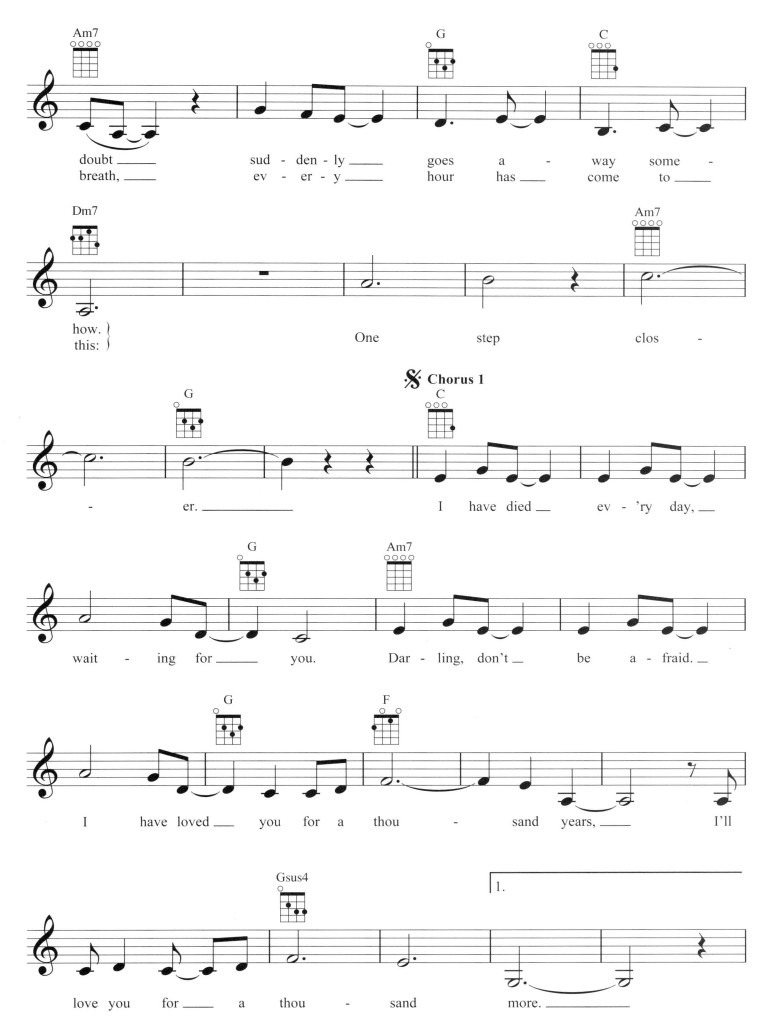

doubt _____ sud - den - ly _____ goes a - way some -
breath, _____ ev - er - y _____ hour has _____ come to

how.)
this:)   One   step   clos -

𝄋 **Chorus 1**

- er. _____ I have died __ ev - 'ry day, __

wait - ing for _____ you. Dar - ling, don't __ be a - fraid. __

I have loved ___ you for a thou - sand years, _____ I'll

1.

love you for _____ a thou - sand more. _____

Fmaj7

more. _____

2., 3.
G

Chorus 2
C   **G**

_____ And all a-long ___ I be-lieved ___ I would find ___ you.

Am7   **G**

Time has brought ___ your heart to me; ___ I have loved ___ you for a

F

thou - sand years, _____ I'll love you for ___ a

To Coda ⊕

Gsus4   **C**   **G**   **Interlude**
                                                           C

thou - sand more. _____

Am7

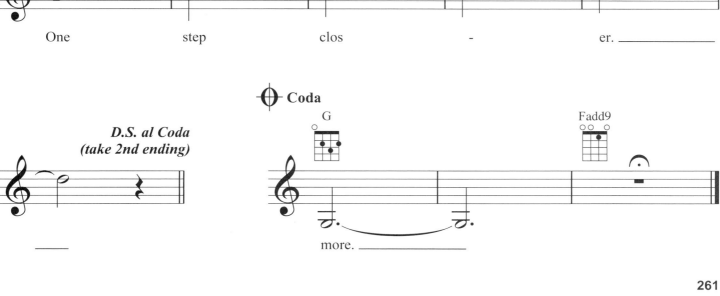

Wake Me Up

Words and Music by Aloe Blacc, Tim Bergling and Michael Einziger

- ver,   when I'm wis - er and I'm old - er. _____   All this

To Coda

time I was find - in' ___ my - self _____ { and I _____ { and I, _____

did - n't know I ___ was   lost. _____

Verse

2. I _____ tried car - ry - ing ___ the weight ___ of ___ the world, _

but I on - ly have ___ two   hands. _____

Hope I get ___ a chance ___ to trav - el ___ the world, _

but I don't have __ an - y plans. _____

Wish that I ___ could stay ___ for - ev - er this young. _____

Not a - fraid ___ to close ___ my eyes. _____

Life's a game _____ made _ for ev - 'ry - one

and love is the prize. _____ So wake me

I did - n't know ___ I ____ was lost. _____

What Makes You Beautiful

Words and Music by Savan Kotecha, Rami Yacoub and Carl Falk

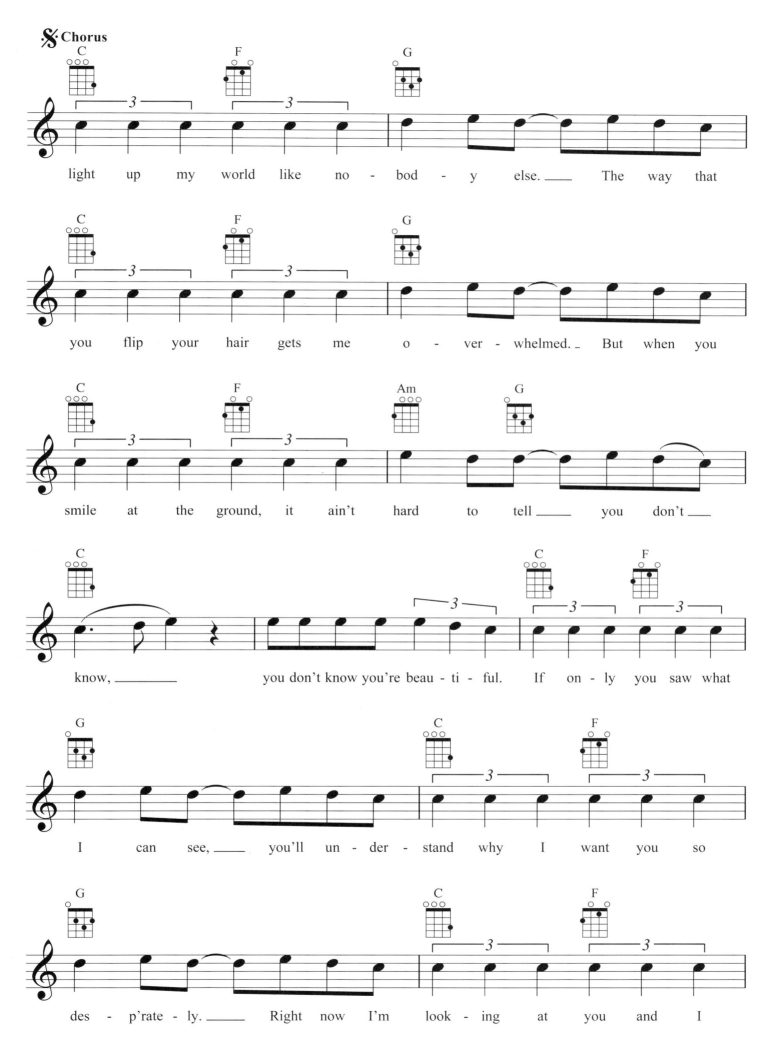

can't be - lieve _ you don't _ know, _____ you don't know you're beau - ti - ful.

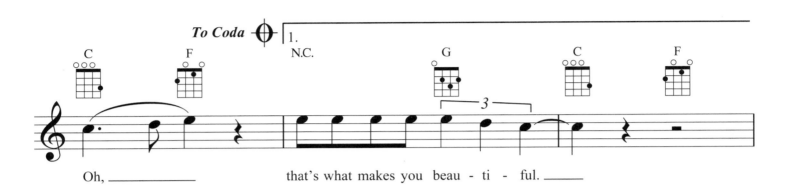

Oh, _____ that's what makes you beau - ti - ful. _____

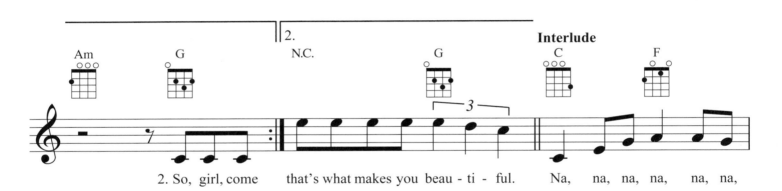

2. So, girl, come that's what makes you beau - ti - ful. Na, na, na, na, na, na,

na, na, ___ na. Na, na, na, na, na, na.

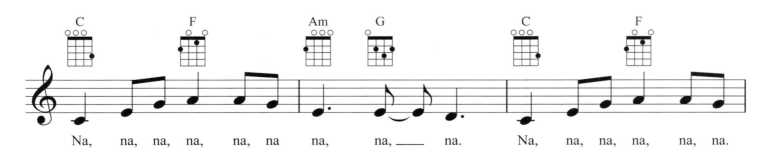

Na, na, na, na, na, na na, na, ___ na. Na, na, na, na, na, na.

Ba - by, you light up my world like no - bod - y else. __ The way that

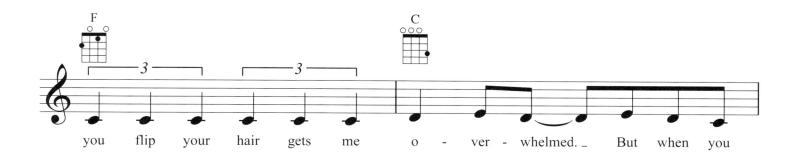

you flip your hair gets me o - ver - whelmed. __ But when you

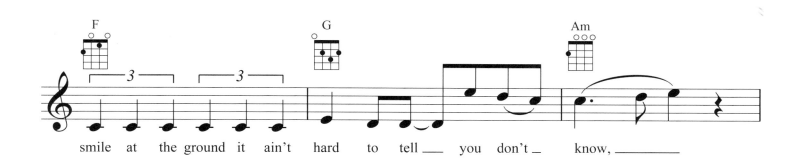

smile at the ground it ain't hard to tell __ you don't __ know, _____

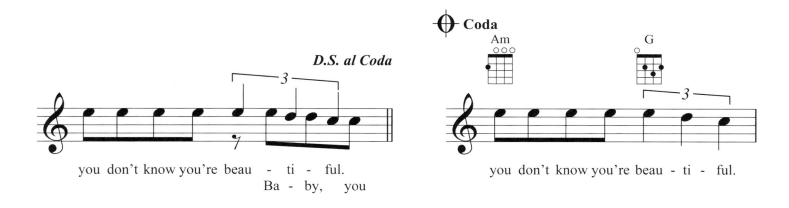

you don't know you're beau - ti - ful.
Ba - by, you

you don't know you're beau - ti - ful.

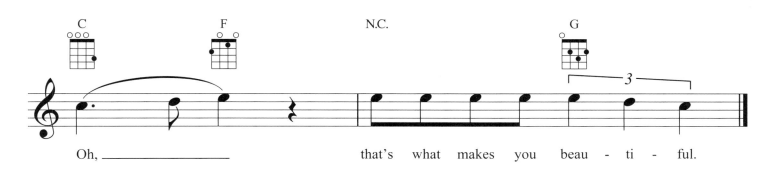

Oh, _____

that's what makes you beau - ti - ful.

The Best Collections for Ukulele

The Best Songs Ever

70 songs have now been arranged for ukulele. Includes: Always • Bohemian Rhapsody • Memory • My Favorite Things • Over the Rainbow • Piano Man • What a Wonderful World • Yesterday • You Raise Me Up • and more.

00282413 . . . . $17.99

Campfire Songs for Ukulele

30 favorites to sing as you roast marshmallows and strum your uke around the campfire. Includes: God Bless the U.S.A. • Hallelujah • The House of the Rising Sun • I Walk the Line • Puff the Magic Dragon • Wagon Wheel • You Are My Sunshine • and more.

00129170 . . . . $14.99

The Daily Ukulele

compiled and arranged by
Liz and Jim Beloff
Strum a different song everyday with easy arrangements of 365 of your favorite songs in one big songbook! Includes favorites by the Beatles, Beach Boys, and Bob Dylan, folk songs, pop songs, kids' songs, Christmas carols, and Broadway and Hollywood tunes, all with a spiral binding for ease of use.

00240356 . . . . $39.99

The Daily Ukulele – Leap Year Edition

366 More Songs for Better Living
compiled and arranged by
Liz and Jim Beloff
An amazing second volume with 366 MORE songs for you to master each day of a leap year! Includes: Ain't No Sunshine • Calendar Girl • I Got You Babe • Lean on Me • Moondance • and many, many more.

00240681 . . . . $39.99

Disney Hits for Ukulele

Play 23 of your favorite Disney songs on your ukulele. Includes: The Bare Necessities • Cruella De Vil • Do You Want to Build a Snowman? • Kiss the Girl • Lava • Let It Go • Once upon a Dream • A Whole New World • and more.

00151250 . . . . $14.99

First 50 Songs You Should Play on Ukulele

An amazing collection of 50 accessible, must-know favorites: Edelweiss • Hey, Soul Sister • I Walk the Line • I'm Yours • Imagine • Over the Rainbow • Peaceful Easy Feeling • The Rainbow Connection • Riptide • and many more.

00149250 . . . . $14.99

The Ukulele 4 Chord Songbook

With just 4 chords, you can play 50 hot songs on your ukulele! Songs include: Brown Eyed Girl • Do Wah Diddy Diddy • Hey Ya! • Ho Hey • Jessie's Girl • Let It Be • One Love • Stand by Me • Toes • With or Without You • and many more.

00142050 . . . . $16.99

Simple Songs for Ukulele

50 favorites for standard G-C-E-A ukulele tuning, including: All Along the Watchtower • Can't Help Falling in Love • Don't Worry, Be Happy • Ho Hey • I'm Yours • King of the Road • Sweet Home Alabama • You Are My Sunshine • and more.

00156815 . . . . $14.99

Top Hits of 2019

Strum your favorite songs of 2019 on the uke. Includes: Bad Guy (Billie Eilish) • I Don't Care (Ed Sheeran & Justin Bieber) • ME! (Taylor Swift) • Old Town Road (Remix) (Lil Nas X feat. Billy Ray Cyrus) • Senorita (Shawn Mendes & Camila Cabello) • Someone You Loved (Lewis Capaldi) • and more.

00302274 . . . . $14.99

The Ukulele 3 Chord Songbook

If you know three chords, you can play these 50 great hits! Songs include: Bad Moon Rising • A Boy Named Sue • King of the Road • Leaving on a Jet Plane • Shelter from the Storm • Time for Me to Fly • Twist and Shout • and many more.

00141143 . . . . $16.99

The Ultimate Ukulele Fake Book

Uke enthusiasts will love this giant, spiral-bound collection of over 400 songs for uke! Includes: Crazy • Dancing Queen • Downtown • Fields of Gold • Happy • Hey Jude • 7 Years • Summertime • Thinking Out Loud • Thriller • Wagon Wheel • and more.

00175500 . . . . $45.00

Ukulele – The Most Requested Songs

Strum & Sing Series
Cherry Lane Music
Nearly 50 favorites all expertly arranged for ukulele! Includes: Bubbly • Build Me Up, Buttercup • Cecilia • Georgia on My Mind • Kokomo • L-O-V-E • Your Body Is a Wonderland • and dozens more.

02501453 . . . . $14.99

Prices, contents, and availability subject to change.